Language: Usage and Practice, Hi

Contents

Contents continued

Contents *continued*

Unit 4: Capitalization and Punctuation

Unit 5: Composition

Language: Usage and Practice HS, SV 1419027867

The *Language: Usage and Practice* series meets many needs.

- It is designed for students who require additional practice in the basics of effective writing and speaking.
- It provides focused practice in key grammar, usage, mechanics, and composition areas.
- It helps students gain ownership of essential skills.
- It presents practice exercises in a clear, concise format in a logical sequence.
- It allows for easy and independent use.

The *Language: Usage and Practice* lessons are organized into a series of units arranged in a logical sequence.

- vocabulary
- sentences
- grammar and usage
- mechanics of capitalization and punctuation
- composition skills

The *Language: Usage and Practice* lessons are carefully formatted for student comfort.

- Systematic, focused attention is given to just one carefully selected skill at a time.
- Rules are clearly stated at the beginning of each lesson and are illustrated with examples.
- Key terms are introduced in bold type.
- Meaningful practice exercises reinforce the skill.
- Each lesson is clearly labeled, and directions are clear and uncomplicated.

The *Language: Usage and Practice* series stresses the application of language principles in a variety of ways.

- Students are asked to match, circle, or underline elements in a predetermined sentence.
- Students are also asked to use what they have learned in an original sentence or in rewriting a sentence.

The *Language: Usage and Practice* series is designed for independent use.

- Because the format is logical and consistent and the vocabulary is carefully controlled, students can use *Language: Usage and Practice* with a high degree of independence.
- Copies of the worksheets can be given to individuals, pairs of students, or small groups for completion.
- Worksheets can be used in the language arts center.
- Worksheets can be given as homework for reviewing and reinforcing skills.

The *Language: Usage and Practice* series provides writing instruction.

- The process approach to teaching writing provides success for most students.
- *Language: Usage and Practice* provides direct support for the teaching of composition and significantly enhances those strategies and techniques commonly associated with the process-writing approach.
- Each book includes a composition unit that provides substantial work with composition skills, such as writing topic sentences, selecting supporting details, taking notes, writing reports, and revising and proofreading.
- Also included in the composition unit is practice with various prewriting activities, such as clustering and brainstorming, which play an important part in process writing.
- The composition lessons are presented in the same rule-plus-practice format as in the other units.

The *Language: Usage and Practice* series includes additional features.

- **Unit Tests**   Use the unit tests to check student progress and prepare students for standardized tests.
- **Sequential Support**   The content of each unit is repeated and expanded in subsequent levels as highlighted in the skills correlation chart on pages 5 and 6.
- **Assessment**   Use the Assessment on pages 7–10 to determine the skills your students need to practice.
- **Language Terms**   Provide each student with a copy of the list of language terms on the inside back cover to keep for reference throughout the year.
- **Small-Group Activities**   Use the worksheets as small-group activities to give students the opportunity to work cooperatively.

The *Language: Usage and Practice* series is a powerful tool!

**The activities use a variety of strategies to maintain student interest.
Watch your students' language improve as skills are
applied in structured, relevant practice!**

Language: Usage and Practice HS, SV 1419027867

Skills Correlation

	1	2	3	4	5	6	7	8	High School
Vocabulary									
Rhyming Words	■	■							
Synonyms and Antonyms	■	■	■	■	■	■	■	■	■
Homonyms	■	■	■	■	■	■	■	■	■
Multiple Meanings/Homographs	■	■	■	■	■	■	■	■	■
Prefixes and Suffixes		■	■	■	■	■	■	■	■
Compound Words		■	■	■	■	■	■	■	■
Contractions		■	■	■	■	■	■	■	■
Idioms						■	■	■	■
Connotation/Denotation					■	■	■	■	
Sentences									
Word Order in Sentences	■	■		■					
Recognizing Sentences and Sentence Types	■	■	■	■	■	■	■	■	■
Subjects and Predicates	■	■	■	■	■	■	■	■	■
Compound/Complex Sentences			■	■	■	■	■	■	■
Sentence Combining		■	■	■	■	■	■	■	■
Run-on Sentences			■	■	■	■	■	■	■
Independent and Subordinate Clauses							■	■	■
Compound Subjects and Predicates	■			■	■	■	■	■	■
Direct and Indirect Objects					■		■	■	■
Inverted Word Order						■			■
Grammar and Usage									
Common and Proper Nouns	■	■	■	■	■	■	■	■	■
Singular and Plural Nouns	■	■	■	■	■	■	■	■	■
Possessive Nouns			■	■	■	■	■	■	■
Appositives					■	■	■		
Verbs and Verb Tense	■	■	■	■	■	■	■	■	■
Regular/Irregular Verbs	■	■	■	■	■	■	■	■	■
Subject/Verb Agreement	■	■	■	■	■	■	■	■	■
Verb Phrases						■	■	■	■
Transitive and Intransitive Verbs							■	■	
Verbals: Gerunds, Participles, and Infinitives							■	■	■
Active and Passive Voice							■	■	
Mood								■	
Pronouns	■	■	■	■	■	■	■		■
Antecedents					■		■	■	■
Articles	■	■	■		■	■			
Adjectives	■	■	■	■	■	■	■	■	■
Correct Word Usage (e.g., may/can, sit/set)	■		■	■	■	■	■	■	■
Adverbs			■	■	■	■	■	■	■
Prepositions					■	■	■	■	
Prepositional Phrases					■	■	■	■	
Conjunctions					■	■	■		■
Interjections					■	■			
Double Negatives								■	■
Capitalization and Punctuation									
Capitalization: First Word in Sentence	■	■	■	■	■	■	■	■	■
Capitalization: Proper Nouns	■	■	■	■	■	■	■	■	■
Capitalization: in Letters			■	■	■		■	■	■
Capitalization: Abbreviations and Titles			■	■	■	■	■	■	■
Capitalization: Proper Adjectives					■	■	■	■	■

Language: Usage and Practice HS, SV 1419027867

	1	2	3	4	5	6	7	8	High School
Capitalization and Punctuation (cont'd)									
End Punctuation	■	■	■	■	■	■	■	■	■
Commas		■	■	■	■	■	■	■	■
Apostrophes in Contractions		■	■	■	■	■	■	■	■
Apostrophes in Possessives			■	■	■	■	■	■	■
Quotation Marks			■	■	■	■	■	■	■
Colons/Semicolons					■	■	■	■	■
Hyphens						■	■	■	■
Composition									
Expanding Sentences			■		■	■	■	■	
Paragraphs: Topic Sentence (main idea)		■	■	■	■	■	■	■	■
Paragraphs: Supporting Details		■	■	■	■	■	■	■	■
Order in Paragraphs			■	■	■	■	■		■
Writing Process:									
Audience				■	■	■	■	■	
Topic			■	■	■	■	■	■	
Outlining				■		■	■	■	
Clustering/Brainstorming					■		■	■	
Note Taking						■			
Revising/Proofreading					■	■	■	■	
Types of Writing:									
Poem	■								
Letter	■	■	■			■			
"How-to" Paragraph			■						
Invitation			■						
Telephone Message			■						
Conversation				■					
Narrative Paragraph				■					
Comparing and Contrasting					■				
Descriptive Paragraph					■				
Report						■			
Interview							■		
Persuasive Composition								■	
Readiness/Study Skills									
Grouping	■		■						
Letters of Alphabet	■								
Listening	■	■							
Making Comparisons	■	■							
Organizing Information		■	■						
Following Directions	■	■	■	■	■				
Alphabetical Order	■	■	■	■	■				
Using a Dictionary:									
Definitions		■	■			■	■	■	
Guide Words/Entry Words		■	■	■	■	■	■	■	
Syllables and Pronunciation						■	■	■	
Multiple Meanings		■	■			■	■	■	
Word Origins						■	■	■	
Parts of a Book		■					■		
Using the Library						■	■	■	
Using Encyclopedias				■	■	■	■	■	
Using Reference Books						■	■	■	
Using the *Readers' Guide*							■	■	
Using Tables, Charts, Graphs, and Diagrams								■	
Choosing Appropriate Sources						■	■	■	

www.harcourtschoolsupply.com
© Harcourt Achieve Inc. All rights reserved.

Skills Correlation
Language: Usage and Practice HS, SV 1419027867

Name _____ Date _____

Assessment

✸ **Write S before each pair of synonyms, A before each pair of antonyms, and H before each pair of homonyms.**

_____ **1.** fearless, brave   _____ **3.** gentle, rough

_____ **2.** pane, pain   _____ **4.** calm, peaceful

✸ **Write the homograph for the pair of meanings.**

5. _____ **a.** air movement   **b.** to tighten a spring

✸ **Write P before each word with a prefix, S before each word with a suffix, and C before each compound word.**

_____ **6.** foolish   _____ **9.** misinform

_____ **7.** roadblock   _____ **10.** sidewalk

_____ **8.** unforgiving   _____ **11.** careful

✸ **Write the words that make up each contraction.**

12. she'd _____ _____   **13.** mustn't _____ _____

✸ **Circle the letter of the idiom that means "spend less money."**

14. a. cut corners   **b.** pull some strings

✸ **Write D before the declarative sentence, IM before the imperative sentence, E before the exclamatory sentence, and IN before the interrogative sentence. Then underline the simple subject and circle the simple predicate in each sentence.**

_____ **15.** Help, my foot is trapped!   _____ **17.** Did you forget our appointment?

_____ **16.** Place your books here.   _____ **18.** All members will meet in this room.

✸ **Write CS before the sentence that has a compound subject and CP before the sentence that has a compound predicate.**

_____ **19.** The cake and bread are kept in the box.

_____ **20.** Taro swims and dives quite well.

✸ **Write CS before the compound sentence, RO before the run-on sentence, and I before the sentence that is in inverted order.**

_____ **21.** I decided on a college, I did many hours of research.

_____ **22.** We can row around the lake, or we can go swimming.

_____ **23.** Over the roof flew the baseball.

✸ **Underline the common nouns and circle the proper nouns in the sentence.**

24. Miss Matson spoke to Jennifer and me about her trip to Los Angeles.

Assessment, p. 2

❊ **Write past, present, or future to show the tense of each underlined verb.**

_____ 25. Mona and I <u>rode</u> the bus to work.

_____ 26. Jack <u>will come</u> home tomorrow morning.

_____ 27. Your phone <u>is</u> broken.

_____ 28. Rosa and I <u>will work</u> until seven o'clock.

❊ **Circle the correct verbs in parentheses to complete each sentence.**

29. Spruce Park (is, are) a great place, and we (is, are) going to have a wonderful time.

30. Steve (drove, will drive) his car after it has been repaired.

31. The flight attendants will (teach, learn) us the safety rules of the airplane.

32. (Sit, Set) the glass beside the sink where the plates are (sitting, setting).

❊ **Write SP before the sentence that has a subject pronoun, OP before the sentence that has an object pronoun, PP before the sentence that has a possessive pronoun, and IP before the sentence that has an indefinite pronoun. Circle the pronoun in each sentence.**

_____ 33. Somebody should call the police.

_____ 34. Alicia told Katie and me about the promotion.

_____ 35. The dog scratched its side repeatedly.

_____ 36. Chris and I are going to the supply room.

❊ **Underline the pronoun. Circle its antecedent.**

37. Gilberto did his taxes before the deadline.

38. Bill and Ariana are on their way to catch the plane.

❊ **Write adjective or adverb to describe the underlined word.**

_____ 39. The man rested on the <u>green</u> sofa.

_____ 40. I answer my mail <u>promptly</u>.

_____ 41. That was the <u>most hilarious</u> movie I've ever seen.

_____ 42. Traffic seems <u>light</u> today.

_____ 43. The <u>dreary</u> rain fell against the windows.

_____ 44. Tina <u>anxiously</u> awaited the arrival of the package.

❊ **Underline each prepositional phrase twice. Circle each preposition. Underline the conjunction once.**

45. The party was held in the largest room of the hotel, and many people were in attendance.

46. The house on the corner must sell quickly, or the owner will take it off the market.

Name _____   Date _____

Assessment, p. 3

 Identify the part of speech of each underlined word. Darken the circle by your answer.

47. Abdellah decided to have dinner <u>at</u> his friend's house.
    - Ⓐ preposition
    - Ⓑ pronoun
    - Ⓒ adverb
    - Ⓓ conjunction

48. The waitress <u>quickly</u> handed me a menu.
    - Ⓐ pronoun
    - Ⓑ adverb
    - Ⓒ adjective
    - Ⓓ preposition

49. Tamara <u>and</u> Richard worked together on the crossword puzzle.
    - Ⓐ conjunction
    - Ⓑ adjective
    - Ⓒ pronoun
    - Ⓓ adverb

50. We have really enjoyed <u>our</u> visit with you.
    - Ⓐ noun
    - Ⓑ adverb
    - Ⓒ conjunction
    - Ⓓ pronoun

51. Ken told <u>himself</u> not to worry about the plans for the trip.
    - Ⓐ adverb
    - Ⓑ pronoun
    - Ⓒ adjective
    - Ⓓ preposition

52. I'd like to stay here longer, <u>but</u> I'm afraid I'll miss the bus.
    - Ⓐ pronoun
    - Ⓑ preposition
    - Ⓒ adverb
    - Ⓓ conjunction

 Darken the circle by the answer that best completes each sentence.

53. _____ more dishes to wash.
    - Ⓐ There is
    - Ⓑ There are
    - Ⓒ There was

54. What _____ will the weather have on your plans?
    - Ⓐ accept
    - Ⓑ affect
    - Ⓒ effect

55. _____ did Mary see at the grocery store?
    - Ⓐ Who
    - Ⓑ Whom
    - Ⓒ Them

56. Those cats don't _____ jump over that fence.
    - Ⓐ anyway
    - Ⓑ ever
    - Ⓒ never

57. Will you _____ my apology?
    - Ⓐ except
    - Ⓑ accept
    - Ⓒ affect

58. _____ shoes are very stylish.
    - Ⓐ This
    - Ⓑ That
    - Ⓒ These

59. There isn't _____ paper left.
    - Ⓐ none
    - Ⓑ any
    - Ⓒ no

60. The sunlight _____ his eyes.
    - Ⓐ excepts
    - Ⓑ effects
    - Ⓒ affects

Assessment, p. 4

✳ Check the capitalization in each sentence. Write C for correct capitalization or I for incorrect capitalization.

_____ **61.** The Middle East is an important oil-producing region of the world.

_____ **62.** Each year thousands of people visit the golden gate bridge in San francisco.

_____ **63.** Does he work for Joe's Household Appliance Company?

_____ **64.** I visited several islands in Hawaii, including maui and oahu, on my trip.

✳ Check how the commas, semicolons, and quotation marks are used in each sentence. Write C for correct punctuation or I for incorrect punctuation.

_____ **65.** "I want to learn to play tennis, but I can't afford those lessons, said Chen."

_____ **66.** "I'll teach you how to volley," said Deborah, "but I'm not good at serving."

_____ **67.** "Well, if you have time, we could practice after work," said Chen.

_____ **68.** "Great said Deborah, "I'll bring my racket tomorrow and we can start."

✳ Read each sentence and decide what capitalization and punctuation are needed. Darken the circle by your answer.

69. Lindsey doesnt want to study algebra geometry or consumer math

Ⓐ Lindsey doesnt want to study algebra geometry, or consumer math.

Ⓑ Lindsey doesn't want to study algebra geometry or consumer math.

Ⓒ Lindsey doesn't want to study algebra, geometry, or consumer math.

70. Dogs are sociable pets cats are independent pets

Ⓐ Dogs are sociable pets, cats are independent pets.

Ⓑ Dogs are sociable pets; cats are independent pets.

Ⓒ Dogs are sociable pets: cats are independent pets.

✳ Read the paragraph below. Then circle the topic sentence and underline only the supporting details.

71.   Phonograph records have changed over the years. Thomas Edison made them from glass, and he used sound waves to carve the grooves into the records. Edison also invented electricity. Later, phonograph records were made of plastic or vinyl. Today's compact discs are made of aluminum.

✳ Number the sentences in order with the topic sentence first.

_____ **72.** Then they walk to find water, and they drink their fill.

_____ **73.** An elephant herd walks and eats most of the day.

_____ **74.** The elephants wake early to graze before it gets too hot.

_____ **75.** Finally, they lie down and sleep.

Name _____   Date _____

Synonyms and Antonyms

- A **synonym** is a word that has the same or nearly the same meaning as another word.
  EXAMPLES: happiness—joy   locate—find

 Write a synonym for each word. Use a dictionary if needed.

1. small _____little_____

2. swiftly _____

3. weary _____

4. beautiful _____

5. large _____

6. awful _____

7. automobile _____

8. employment _____

9. lift _____

10. leap _____

11. pleasant _____

12. assist _____

13. leave _____

14. inquire _____

15. children _____

16. artificial _____

17. well-known _____

18. swap _____

19. house _____

20. simple _____

21. carpet _____

22. listen _____

23. chair _____

24. street _____

- An **antonym** is a word that has the opposite meaning of another word.
  EXAMPLES: old—new   came—went

 Write an antonym for each word. Use a dictionary if needed.

25. failure _____success_____

26. absent _____

27. before _____

28. slow _____

29. all _____

30. remember _____

31. love _____

32. enemy _____

33. early _____

34. sharp _____

35. thick _____

36. tall _____

37. crooked _____

38. happy _____

39. subtract _____

40. ugly _____

41. false _____

42. harmful _____

43. raise _____

44. together _____

45. idle _____

46. smooth _____

47. dark _____

48. narrow _____

Unit 1: Vocabulary
Language: Usage and Practice HS, SV 1419027867

Name _____ Date _____

Homonyms

> • A **homonym** is a word that sounds the same as another word but has a different spelling and a different meaning.
> • A homonym is also known as a **homophone**.
>   EXAMPLES: aisle—I'll—isle   course—coarse   flower—flour

 Underline the correct homonym(s) in each sentence. Use a dictionary if needed.

1. When Matt gave Elise her (wring, <u>ring</u>), did he (<u>wring</u>, ring) his hands nervously?

2. The boat with the red and white (sale, sail) is for (sale, sail).

3. Dustin likes to (brows, browse) around in hardware stores.

4. We spent several (days, daze) at an old-fashioned (in, inn).

5. Have you met my (son, sun) before?

6. A large (boulder, bolder) rolled down the mountainside.

7. That fisherman on the (pier, peer) seems to (pier, peer) longingly out to (sea, see).

8. They asked the bank for a (lone, loan).

9. We drove four miles in a foggy (missed, mist).

10. I'm buying a bright (red, read) or (blew, blue) umbrella before the next (rein, rain).

11. Jack (threw, through) the ball (threw, through) the garage window.

12. We (buy, by) our fish fresh from the market (buy, by) the shore.

13. We have an (hour, our) to get to (hour, our) seats in the middle (aisle, isle, I'll).

14. Who is the (principal, principle) of your friend's school?

15. The U.S. Congress (meats, meets) in the (Capitol, Capital) building.

16. During the parade, the rider (lead, led) her (hoarse, horse) by the (rains, reins).

17. She stepped on the (breaks, brakes) suddenly.

18. (Their, There) are too many people in this elevator.

19. The office manager arranged our desks in a (strait, straight) line.

20. We are not (allowed, aloud) to drink coffee near the computer.

21. Will they have to (toe, tow) Kareem's car?

22. Has the supervisor (shone, shown) you how to operate this machine yet?

23. On your (way, weigh) to the mailroom, find out how much the crates (way, weigh).

24. Don't forget (to, too, two) go by the warehouse in (to, too, two) hours, (to, too, two).

25. Who broke this (pane, pain) in the window?

26. Laurie (knew, new) how to use the (knew, new) computer.

27. Juan and Luis spent a week at (there, their, they're) cousin's house.

28. Those boys (ate, eight) (ate, eight) of the apples we had just bought.

29. I like to walk by the (see, sea) in the morning when I can (see, sea) the sun rising.

30. If you are (board, bored) with painting, help me saw this (board, bored) in two.

Language: Usage and Practice HS, SV 1419027867

Name _____ Date _____

Homographs

- A **homograph** is a word that looks the same as another word but has a different meaning and sometimes a different pronunciation.
- Homographs are spelled alike.
    EXAMPLES: Saw means "have seen" or "a tool used for cutting."
    Bow means "to bend the body in recognition" or
    "a decorative knot in a ribbon."

 Circle the letter of the definition for the underlined homograph as it is used in the sentence.

1. Sara jumped when she heard the loud <u>bangs</u> of the backfiring car.

   a. a fringe of hair   **b.** loud noises

2. She grabbed a stick to <u>arm</u> herself against the growling dog.

   a. a part of the body   **b.** to take up a weapon

3. The hound's continuous <u>bark</u> awoke the family.

   a. the noise a dog makes   **b.** outside covering of a tree

4. Stir the pancake <u>batter</u> for three minutes.

   a. a person at bat   **b.** a mixture used in cooking

5. The <u>checkers</u> are working as fast as they can.

   a. pieces of a board game   **b.** cashiers

6. He heated a <u>can</u> of tomato soup for his supper.

   a. a metal container   **b.** to be able to

7. I tried to <u>hide</u> the birthday cake for Jean's surprise party.

   a. an animal skin   **b.** to put out of sight

8. If you <u>desert</u> me now, I'll never finish cleaning the garage.

   a. dry, sandy place   **b.** to leave someone behind; to abandon

9. Leave the keys on the kitchen <u>counter</u> before you go to work.

   a. a long table or cabinet top   **b.** a person or thing that counts

10. The <u>jar</u> was filled with homemade strawberry jam.

    a. a glass container   **b.** to jolt or shake

 Write the homograph for each pair of meanings below. The first letter of each word is given for you.

11. **a.** money paid as a penalty   **b.** better than average; clear and bright   f _____

12. **a.** a metal fastener   **b.** a sound made with fingers   s _____

13. **a.** in good health   **b.** hole in the earth to tap water   w _____

14. **a.** festival or carnival   **b.** honest; not partial to someone   f _____

15. **a.** device to fasten a door   **b.** curl or ringlet of hair   l _____

Language: Usage and Practice HS, SV 1419027867

Name _____   Date _____

Prefixes

- A **prefix** is a letter or letters added to the beginning of a word that change the meaning of the word.
- Here are some common prefixes and their meanings:

prefix	meaning	prefix	meaning
in	not, without	re	again
dis	not	fore	before
un	not, reverse	pre	before
im	not	mis	not, wrong, or wrongly
non	not	with	from, against

EXAMPLE: happy + <u>un</u> = **unhappy**, meaning "not happy"

 Write a new word by adding the prefix <u>un</u>, <u>im</u>, <u>non</u>, or <u>mis</u> to the word in parentheses in each sentence. Then write the meaning of the new word on the line below the sentence. Use a dictionary if needed.

1. It is _____ impractical _____ (practical) to put a new monkey into a cage with other monkeys.

   _____ not practical _____

2. The monkeys might _____ (behave) with a newcomer among them.

   _____

3. They will feel quite _____ (easy) for a number of days or even weeks.

   _____

4. Even if the new monkey is _____ (violent) in nature, the others may harm it.

   _____

5. Sometimes animal behavior can be quite _____ (usual).

   _____

 Underline each prefix. Then write the meaning of the word with a prefix.

6. <u>un</u>expected guest ___ not expected ___

7. really disappear _____

8. disagree often _____

9. misspell a name _____

10. preview a movie _____

11. reenter a room _____

12. misplace a shoe _____

13. impossible job _____

14. nonstop work _____

15. unimportant day _____

16. insane story _____

17. prejudge a person _____

Language: Usage and Practice HS, SV 1419027867

Suffixes

- A **suffix** is a letter or letters added to the end of a word that change the meaning of the word.
- Here are some common suffixes and their meanings:

suffix	meaning	suffix	meaning
less	without	ist	one skilled in
ish	the qualities of	tion	art of
ous	full of	ful	full of
en	to make	al	pertaining to
hood	state of being	able, ible	able to be
ward	in the direction of	ly, y	like, pertaining to
ness	quality of being	or, er	person having to do with
ment	a means of being	like	similar to

- Sometimes you need to change the spelling of a word to add a suffix.

EXAMPLES: worth + <u>less</u> = **worthless** "without worth"
home + <u>ward</u> = **homeward** "in the direction of home"
happy + <u>ness</u> = **happiness** "state of being happy"

 Write a new word by adding a suffix to the end of the word in parentheses in each sentence. Then write the meaning of the new word. Use each suffix only once.

1. Switzerland is a _____ <u>mountainous</u> _____ country. (mountain)

   _____ <u>full of mountains</u> _____

2. When you go hiking, wear _____ walking shoes. (comfort)

   _____

3. In Marquette, Michigan, more than half the days in a year are _____. (snow)

   _____

4. My sister wants to be a kindergarten _____. (teach)

   _____

5. Is that mechanic _____ about foreign cars? (knowledge)

   _____

 Underline each suffix. Then write the meaning of the word with a suffix.

6. break<u>able</u> toy _____ <u>able to be broken</u>

7. endless waves _____

8. hazardous waste _____

9. regrettable mistake _____

10. poisonous snake _____

11. dependable trains _____

12. humorous song _____

13. tearful good-bye _____

14. bumpy ride _____

15. careless driver _____

16. natural food _____

17. dirty job _____

Contractions

> • A **contraction** is a word formed by joining two other words.
> • An **apostrophe** is used to show where a letter or letters have been left out.
>   EXAMPLES: had + not = **hadn't**   she + is = **she's**
> • <u>Won't</u> is an exception.
>   EXAMPLE: will + not = **won't**

 **Write the contraction for each group of words. Use an apostrophe.**

1. did not _____ didn't _____

11. they have _____

2. you will _____

12. would not _____

3. we are _____

13. will not _____

4. is not _____

14. you would _____

5. who is _____

15. were not _____

6. had not _____

16. there is _____

7. I will _____

17. could not _____

8. we have _____

18. I have _____

9. it is _____

19. she will _____

10. do not _____

20. they are _____

 **Underline each contraction. Write the words that make up the contraction on the line.**

21. We're looking at used cars very carefully.   _____ We are _____

22. We'll buy one if we can afford it.   _____

23. If it's in good condition, my husband wants to take it home today.   _____

24. He's interested in starting his own car service.   _____

25. I think he'll like working with automobiles.   _____

26. Ana loves cooking for friends; she's a great cook.   _____

27. She'd like to be a professional chef.   _____

28. She would've liked going to cooking school part-time.   _____

29. But there weren't any evening classes offered nearby.   _____

30. I've heard she found a school with classes on the weekends.   _____

Name _____   Date _____

Compound Words

- A **compound word** is a word made of two or more words.
- The meaning of a compound word is related to the meanings of the smaller words.
    - EXAMPLE: sail + boat = **sailboat**   "a boat using a sail for power"
- Some compound words become one word. Some compound words remain separate words. Some compound words are hyphenated.
- A dictionary shows how a compound word is written.
    - EXAMPLES: baseball   grandchild   hairbrush
    -                    ice cream   slow-paced   air-condition

 Use the words in the box as often as you need to make compound words.

sand	fall	paper	color	home	water	room	play
made	field	under	come	out	stand	mate	back

1. _____sandpaper_____   7. _____

2. _____   8. _____

3. _____   9. _____

4. _____   10. _____

5. _____   11. _____

6. _____   12. _____

 Answer the questions about compound words.

13. The word <u>books</u> sometimes refers to "financial accounts."

    What is a <u>bookkeeper</u>? ____person who keeps the financial accounts_____

14. <u>Ferry</u> means "to transport across a body of water."

    What is a <u>ferryboat</u>? _____

15. A <u>lord</u> is "a person who has great authority over something."

    What is a <u>landlord</u>? _____

16. A <u>toll</u> is "a charge for permission to pass over a bridge or along a highway."

    What is a <u>tollbooth</u>? _____

17. <u>Rock</u> means "to move back and forth."

    What is a <u>rocking chair</u>? _____

Language: Usage and Practice HS, SV 1419027867

Idioms

> • An **idiom** is an expression that doesn't literally mean what it says.
>   EXAMPLES: **Lend a hand** doesn't literally mean "let someone borrow a part
>   of the body"; it means "give someone help."
>   **Hit the road** doesn't literally mean "slap the street"; it means
>   "leave" or "go away."

 Match each underlined idiom to its meaning. Write the letter of the answer on the line.

a. in a risky situation	**f.** continue to have hope
b. do less than one should	**g.** listening with all one's attention
c. admit to saying the wrong thing	**h.** teasing someone
d. act without an exact plan; improvise	**i.** accept defeat
e. spend money carefully	**j.** meet by chance

_____ 1. Brianne hoped to <u>run across</u> some old friends at the ball game.

_____ 2. I was almost ready to <u>throw in the towel</u> when I finally found my keys.

_____ 3. Patricia was <u>pulling your leg</u> when she told you it snowed here last August.

_____ 4. I told my son he was <u>skating on thin ice</u> when he left a mess in the kitchen.

_____ 5. Gina must <u>make ends meet</u> with the money she makes at her part-time job.

_____ 6. Her parents told her, "<u>Keep your chin up</u> when things get difficult."

_____ 7. Although he'd never made pancakes before, José decided to <u>play it by ear</u>.

_____ 8. I was <u>all ears</u> when José told me about those unusual pancakes he made.

_____ 9. I think William would <u>lie down on the job</u> if someone weren't watching him.

_____ 10. He says I'll <u>eat my words</u> when I see how much work he has done.

 Underline the idiom in each sentence. Then write what the idiom really means. If you need help, look up the main word in a dictionary.

11. Antonio and his children don't always <u>see eye to eye</u> on what a clean room is.

_____ agree completely _____

12. He wants them to keep their nose to the grindstone until everything is neatly put away.

_____

13. It really gets his goat when they don't clean under their beds.

_____

14. Antonio hopes they'll turn over a new leaf and do a more thorough job soon.

_____

15. He has to stick to his guns, or they'll never learn to keep their rooms clean.

_____

    Language: Usage and Practice HS, SV 1419027867

Idioms, p. 2

16. And the children won't have to say, "Dad blew his top again."

_____

17. He doesn't beat around the bush when he asks for help from everyone in the family.

_____

18. He doesn't have time to clean up after them; Antonio has to hit the books for night school.

_____

19. He can kick up his heels when he finishes school.

_____

20. The children haven't spilled the beans about the surprise party for him when he graduates.

_____

✳ **Underline the idiom in each sentence. Write what the idiom really means.**

21. If I don't finish this job before next week, I'm going to be <u>in hot water</u>.

_____ in trouble _____

22. Karl was wrong about the car's engine, so he had to eat crow.

_____

23. Eric didn't buy his bus ticket before the rates changed; now it's just water under the bridge.

_____

✳ **Match each underlined word or group of words to an idiom. Write the letter of the answer on the line.**

a. twist me around his little finger	**d.** in the doghouse
b. on cloud nine	**e.** down in the dumps
c. gave me the cold shoulder	**f.** put the shoe on the other foot

____a____ **24.** My dog Julius can <u>completely control me</u>.

_____ **25.** Sometimes he looks so <u>sad</u> I give him extra treats.

_____ **26.** Then he acts <u>unbelievably happy</u>.

_____ **27.** Once when I forgot to take him for a walk, he <u>ignored me</u>.

_____ **28.** I was <u>out of favor</u> with Julius for several days.

_____ **29.** But when I ignore Julius and <u>reverse the situation</u>, he whines pitifully.

✳ **Write a sentence using one of these idioms: <u>on the fence</u>, <u>out to lunch</u>, or <u>up the creek</u>. Then write what the expression really means.**

30. _____

_____

Language: Usage and Practice HS, SV 1419027867

Name _____ Date _____

Unit 1 Test

On the line before each pair of words, write <u>S</u> if they are synonyms, <u>A</u> if they are antonyms, <u>H</u> if they are homonyms, and <u>HG</u> if they are homographs.

_____ **1.** far, close   _____ **6.** rough, smooth   _____ **11.** plane, plain

_____ **2.** discover, find   _____ **7.** ring, ring   _____ **12.** tall, short

_____ **3.** great, grate   _____ **8.** here, hear   _____ **13.** easy, simple

_____ **4.** jar, jar   _____ **9.** talk, speak   _____ **14.** bear, bear

_____ **5.** mistake, error   _____ **10.** aloud, allowed   _____ **15.** together, apart

Underline the prefix or suffix in each phrase below. Then write the meaning of each word that has the prefix or suffix.

16. impossible task _____   **20.** uneasy feeling _____

17. rusty nails _____   **21.** nonviolent protest _____

18. hazardous road _____   **22.** helpless baby _____

19. incomplete work _____   **23.** beautiful scene _____

Write the two words that make up the contraction in each sentence. Then underline the compound word in each sentence and draw a line between the two words that make up each compound word.

24. "Where's the airplane museum?" asked Anne.   _____ _____

25. "I think it's downtown," said Steve.   _____ _____

26. "Isn't that the pilots' headquarters?" asked Justin.   _____ _____

27. "Yes, they're in the same high-rise," said Steve.   _____ _____

28. "Is that the building where you can't see the rooftop?" asked Anne.   _____ _____

Underline the idiom in each sentence. On the line, write what the expression means.

29. He was worried about finishing in time, but I told him to hang in there.

_____

30. Where does Morgan live now? I'd like to get in touch with him again.

_____

     Language: Usage and Practice HS, SV 1419027867

Unit 1 Test, p. 2

Darken the circle by the correct answer to each question.

31. Which pair of words are synonyms?

   Ⓐ end, begin

   Ⓑ to, too

   Ⓒ like, enjoy

32. Which two words make up the contraction haven't?

   Ⓐ had, not

   Ⓑ have, no

   Ⓒ have, not

33. What is the prefix in disappearance?

   Ⓐ appear

   Ⓑ dis

   Ⓒ ance

34. Which pair of words are antonyms?

   Ⓐ aloud, orally

   Ⓑ aloud, allowed

   Ⓒ aloud, silently

35. Which word is a compound word?

   Ⓐ blackbird

   Ⓑ blackness

   Ⓒ blacker

36. Which sentence uses an idiom?

   Ⓐ Gil said we should go to the party.

   Ⓑ Gil said we should go for it.

   Ⓒ Gil said we might go with him.

37. Which word has a suffix but no prefix?

   Ⓐ uncomfortable

   Ⓑ comfortably

   Ⓒ discomfort

38. What is a homonym for missed?

   Ⓐ must

   Ⓑ mist

   Ⓒ most

39. What is the suffix in unhappiness?

   Ⓐ happy

   Ⓑ un

   Ⓒ ness

40. Which sentence uses an idiom?

   Ⓐ I can't find the hammer to hang the picture.

   Ⓑ I can't hang my coat on the hook.

   Ⓒ I can't get the hang of this new game.

41. Which word is a compound word?

   Ⓐ rainless

   Ⓑ rainy

   Ⓒ rainbow

42. Which two words make up the contraction won't?

   Ⓐ will not

   Ⓑ would not

   Ⓒ was not

43. Which word is a compound word?

   Ⓐ shuffling

   Ⓑ shuffleboard

   Ⓒ reshuffled

44. Which pair of words are homonyms?

   Ⓐ bolder, braver

   Ⓑ bolder, bashful

   Ⓒ bolder, boulder

Sentences and Sentence Fragments

- A **sentence** is a group of words that expresses a complete thought.
  EXAMPLE: We found a deserted cabin at the top of the hill.
- A **fragment** is a group of words that does not express a complete thought.
  EXAMPLE: At the top of the hill

✳ Some of the groups of words are sentences, and some are fragments. Write S before each sentence and F before each fragment. Put the correct punctuation at the end of the sentences.

_____ 1. Tomás did not go to the auto show____

_____ 2. By the side of the babbling brook____

_____ 3. I went to the new museum last week____

_____ 4. Mile after mile along the great highway____

_____ 5. Check all work carefully____

_____ 6. Down the narrow aisle of the auditorium____

_____ 7. I have lost my hat____

_____ 8. On our way to work this morning____

_____ 9. Leontyne Price, a famous singer____

_____ 10. We saw Elaine and Sheryl yesterday____

_____ 11. The severe cold of last winter____

_____ 12. Once when I went to New Orleans____

_____ 13. There was a magnificent sunset last night____

_____ 14. He ran home____

_____ 15. My brother and my sister____

_____ 16. Tyler and Matt did a great job____

_____ 17. The cat in our neighbor's yard____

_____ 18. Every year at the state fair____

_____ 19. As we came to the sharp curve in the road____

_____ 20. Just before we were ready____

_____ 21. I heard that you and Ernesto have a new paper route____

_____ 22. Longfellow is called the children's poet____

_____ 23. Into the parking garage____

_____ 24. We washed and waxed the truck____

_____ 25. Through the door and up the stairs____

_____ 26. As quickly as possible____

_____ 27. Jason parked the car on the street____

_____ 28. We had ice cream and fruit for dessert____

Name _____   Date _____

Sentences and Sentence Fragments, p. 2

※ **Some of the groups of words are sentences, and some are fragments. Write S before each sentence and F before each fragment. Put the correct punctuation at the end of the sentences.**

_____ 29. When the hockey season begins____

_____ 30. Last week I helped Menh repair his car____

_____ 31. From the very beginning of the first-aid lessons____

_____ 32. One of the instructors at the Adult Learning Center____

_____ 33. A visiting musician played the organ____

_____ 34. On the way to work this morning____

_____ 35. "I'll be home late tonight," said Leticia____

_____ 36. The blue house at the corner of Maple Street____

_____ 37. After Ava left, the phone rang off the hook____

_____ 38. Speak distinctly and loudly so that you can be heard____

_____ 39. I have finally learned to drive our car____

_____ 40. I think today is Hamid's birthday____

_____ 41. At the very last moment, we were ready____

_____ 42. When you speak in front of people____

_____ 43. The basket of fruit on the table____

_____ 44. Please answer the telephone, Julia____

_____ 45. Hurrying to class because he is late____

_____ 46. The first thing in the morning____

_____ 47. That mistake was costly and unfortunate____

_____ 48. We are planning to make a new doghouse____

_____ 49. The dog chased the cat up the tree____

_____ 50. Daniel Boone was born in Pennsylvania____

_____ 51. The giant cottonwood in our backyard____

_____ 52. Marla, bring my notebook____

_____ 53. On a stool beside the back door____

_____ 54. Sometimes the noise from the street____

_____ 55. Somewhere out of town____

_____ 56. The band played a lively march____

_____ 57. That flight arrived on time____

_____ 58. Was cracked in dozens of places____

_____ 59. In planning our work schedule____

_____ 60. December is the last month of the year____

※ **Choose two fragments from this exercise. Rewrite each fragment as a sentence.**

61. _____

62. _____

Types of Sentences

- A **declarative sentence** makes a statement. It is followed by a period (.).
  EXAMPLE: Insects have six legs.
- An **interrogative sentence** asks a question. It is followed by a question mark (?).
  EXAMPLE: What are you eating?
- An **imperative sentence** expresses a command or request. It is followed by a period (.).
  EXAMPLE: Open the window.
- An **exclamatory sentence** expresses strong emotion. It can also express a command or request that is made with great excitement. It is followed by an exclamation point (!).
  EXAMPLES: The grass is on fire! Hurry over here!

 Before each sentence, write D for declarative, IN for interrogative, IM for imperative, or E for exclamatory. Put the correct punctuation at the end of each sentence.

__IN__ **1.** What do you consider a fair price_?_

_____ **2.** How many people signed a contract____

_____ **3.** Do not leave objects lying on floors and stairways____

_____ **4.** Mary McLeod Bethune was the first black woman to head an agency of the U.S. government____

_____ **5.** What a cold day it is____

_____ **6.** Robert, where have you been____

_____ **7.** Return those books when you finish them____

_____ **8.** I bought this hat in Canada____

_____ **9.** Look at that beautiful sunset____

_____ **10.** Copy each problem accurately____

_____ **11.** Books are storehouses of knowledge____

_____ **12.** My pet bird is loose____

_____ **13.** How do forests help prevent floods____

_____ **14.** Where did we get the word Thursday____

_____ **15.** Listen carefully____

_____ **16.** Rice is the most widely eaten food in the world____

_____ **17.** Don't lose the book____

_____ **18.** Erin's cousins from North Dakota will arrive Monday____

_____ **19.** Did you buy more milk____

_____ **20.** We saw the new snake exhibit at the zoo____

_____ **21.** Put those supplies on that shelf____

_____ **22.** Do you want to help me make bread____

_____ **23.** We're out of flour____

Name _____   Date _____

Types of Sentences, p. 2

 Before each sentence, write <u>D</u> for declarative, <u>IN</u> for interrogative, <u>IM</u> for imperative, or <u>E</u> for exclamatory. Put the correct punctuation at the end of each sentence.

_____ **24.** Look out for those cars____

_____ **25.** Take good care of my dog____

_____ **26.** There are many cotton mills in the southern United States____

_____ **27.** Name the capital of Nevada____

_____ **28.** Hurray, the game is over____

_____ **29.** Draw a map of the continents____

_____ **30.** Geysers were first discovered in Iceland____

_____ **31.** Have you ever been on a roller coaster____

_____ **32.** Sweep the front walk____

_____ **33.** Do not measure people by what they have____

_____ **34.** A great nation is made only by worthy citizens____

_____ **35.** Anna Moffo has sung with many of the major opera companies____

_____ **36.** What is the longest river in the world____

_____ **37.** Oh, you have a new car____

_____ **38.** Andrea, why weren't you at the meeting____

_____ **39.** The organization will elect officers tomorrow____

_____ **40.** Chris, I have a long piece of twine____

_____ **41.** Pierre, fill out your application quickly____

_____ **42.** Everyone will be here by nine o'clock____

_____ **43.** Train yourself to do your work carefully____

_____ **44.** How does a canal lock work____

_____ **45.** Prepare each day's assignment on time____

_____ **46.** Are we going to the game now____

_____ **47.** Who brought these delicious peaches____

_____ **48.** Our guests have arrived____

_____ **49.** What is meant by rotation of crops____

_____ **50.** Please take the patient a glass of water____

_____ **51.** Stop that noise____

_____ **52.** Always stand erect____

_____ **53.** Who arranged these flowers____

 Write four types of sentences that tell about your day. Put the correct punctuation at the end of each sentence.

_____

_____

_____

_____

Unit 2: Sentences
Language: Usage and Practice HS, SV 1419027867

Name _____ Date _____

End Punctuation Marks

> • Use a **period** at the end of a declarative sentence.
>   EXAMPLE: The first U.S. President was George Washington.
> • Use a **question mark** at the end of an interrogative sentence.
>   EXAMPLE: Which U.S. President's picture is on the one-dollar bill?

 Add a period or question mark to end each sentence correctly.

1. Is this road uphill all the way to Edward's house____

2. Los Angeles, Mexico City, and Rome have all been sites of the Olympic Games____

3. How many people were standing in line for tickets____

4. Wisconsin is a beautiful northern state____

5. Pablo, Jacob, Candace, and Ling were chosen to speak at the meeting____

6. Whom did you see, Christina____

7. Haydn, Mozart, Mendelssohn, and Beethoven composed symphonies____

8. The copy machine will be installed tomorrow____

9. Do you think that Napoleon was an able leader____

10. Does your Aunt Louann live nearby____

11. Who wrote this memo about donating blood____

12. We flew from Seattle, Washington, to Vancouver, British Columbia____

13. Ray Avelone is a guest of Mr. and Mrs. McReynolds____

14. Aaron, have you read "The Gift of the Magi" by O. Henry____

15. Where does your uncle's family live____

16. "Snow Time" is a well-known poem____

17. Isn't someone knocking at the door____

18. Didn't Mrs. Burton ask us to meet her at 4:30 this afternoon____

19. In Yellowstone Park, we saw Morning Glory Pool, Handkerchief Pool, and Old Faithful____

20. The greatest library in ancient times was in Alexandria, Egypt____

21. In which bank are the employees' checks deposited____

22. Will Ms. Weston start interviewing applicants at 10:00 A.M.____

23. My father finally got the promotion he had been waiting for____

24. The new software helped us work more efficiently____

25. Isn't Alicia the chairperson of our committee____

26. I've mowed the lawn, pulled the weeds, and raked the leaves____

27. When was the election held____

28. Is El Salvador in Central America____

29. Which do you prefer, coleslaw or salad____

Language: Usage and Practice HS, SV 1419027867

End Punctuation Marks, p. 2

- Use a **period** at the end of an imperative sentence.
  EXAMPLE: Close the door to the attic.
- Use an **exclamation point** at the end of an exclamatory sentence and after words such as Oh and Oops that show strong feeling.
  EXAMPLES: What a great shot!   Oh! I'd love to go with you!

 Add a period or exclamation point where it is needed in each sentence.

30. Address the envelope to Dr. Georgia K. Washington____

31. How nicely dressed you are____

32. Hurry____ The bus is ready to leave____

33. Get some white paint at the hardware store____

34. Shake hands with Mr. D. B. Dooley____

35. Oh, no____ I spilled the orange juice____

36. Help me carry these boxes to the mailroom____

37. What a great view you have from your apartment window____

38. Wipe the counter when you finish eating____

39. Oh, what a beautiful painting____

40. I can't wait until our new apartment is vacant____

41. Please take this to the post office for me____

42. Just look at the size of the fish he caught____

43. Whoa, kids____ Take those muddy shoes off before you come in the house____

44. Get the papers you need from the personnel office____

45. I hope the pictures come out better this time____

46. Answer the telephone, Michelle____

47. Please clean the kitchen____

48. Oh____ I can't believe how late it is____

49. Take this order to the customer in the booth____

50. Take a seat in the waiting area for the doctor____

51. Hurry____ The plane is leaving in a few minutes____

52. I can't miss the flight____

53. Hold that seat for me____

54. Stop____ Stop____ You forgot your ticket____

55. Please slow down____

56. Sit down and put on your seat belt____

57. We're off____

58. Look how small the city is____

59. Obey the captain's orders____

Name _____ Date _____

Complete Subjects and Predicates

- The two main parts of a sentence are the complete subject and the complete predicate.
- The **complete subject** includes all the words that tell who or what the sentence is about.
    - EXAMPLE: **All chickadees** / hunt insect eggs.
- The **complete predicate** includes all the words that state the action or condition of the subject.
    - EXAMPLE: All chickadees / **hunt insect eggs**.

 Draw a line between the complete subject and the complete predicate in each sentence.

1. Amy / built a bird feeder for the backyard.

2. This cleaner will remove paint.

3. Many beautiful waltzes were composed by Johann Strauss.

4. Queen Victoria ruled England for many years.

5. Eighty people are waiting in line for tickets.

6. Marlo's last visit was during the summer.

7. The rocket was soon in orbit.

8. Our last meeting was held in my living room.

9. The farmers are harvesting their wheat.

10. Our new house has six rooms.

11. The heart pumps blood throughout the body.

12. This computer will help you work faster.

13. My best friend has moved to Phoenix, Arizona.

14. A deep silence fell upon the crowd.

15. The police officers were stopping the speeding motorists.

16. The French chef prepared excellent food.

17. My father is a mechanic.

18. José Salazar is running for the city council.

19. Lightning struck a tree in our yard.

20. Magazines about bicycling are becoming very popular.

21. They answered every question honestly during the interview.

22. The gray twilight came before the program ended.

23. Willy has a way with words.

24. That section of the country has many pine forests.

25. We will have a party for Lateshia on Friday.

26. The big truck was stuck in the mud.

Complete Subjects and Predicates, p. 2

 Write a sentence by adding a complete predicate to each complete subject.

27. All of the reporters _____ rushed to interview the winning coach. _____

28. Elephants _____

29. The top of the mountain _____

30. The television programs tonight _____

31. I _____

32. Each of the firefighters _____

33. My truck _____

34. The dam across the river _____

35. Our new van _____

36. You _____

37. The books in our bookcase _____

38. The mountains _____

39. Today's newspaper _____

40. The magazine staff _____

 Write a sentence by adding a complete subject to each complete predicate.

41. _____ Mexico City _____ is the largest city in Mexico.

42. _____ worked in the doctor's office.

43. _____ is a valuable mineral.

44. _____ grow beside the road.

45. _____ traveled day and night.

46. _____ was a great inventor.

47. _____ wrote a letter of complaint.

48. _____ met us at the airport.

49. _____ made ice cream for the company picnic.

50. _____ made a nest in our tree.

51. _____ lives near the shopping center.

52. _____ have a meeting on Saturday.

Simple Subjects and Predicates

- The **simple subject** of a sentence is the main word in the complete subject. The simple subject is a noun or a pronoun. Sometimes the simple subject is also the complete subject.
  - EXAMPLES: The southern **section** of our state / has many forests.
  - **Forests** / are beautiful.
- The **simple predicate** of a sentence is a verb within the complete predicate. The verb may be made up of one word or more than one word.
  - EXAMPLES: Dogs / **have** good hearing.   Martin / **is going**.

 Draw a line between the complete subject and the complete predicate in each sentence. Underline the simple subject once and the simple predicate twice.

1. The different <u>meanings</u> for that word / <u>cover</u> half of a dictionary page.

2. A valuable oil is made from peanuts.

3. A beautiful highway winds through the Catskill Mountains.

4. The lady in the black dress studied the painting for more than an hour.

5. The meadowlark builds its nest on the ground.

6. A rare Chinese vase was on display.

7. Many stories have been written about the old Spanish Main.

8. His answer to the question was incorrect.

9. Every sentence should begin with a capital letter.

10. All of the group went on a hike.

11. In Norway, a narrow inlet of the sea between cliffs is called a fjord.

12. The Dutch grew large fields of tulips and hyacinths.

13. The two U.S. treasury mints are located in Philadelphia and Denver.

14. Benjamin Franklin's *Poor Richard's Almanac* is filled with wise sayings.

15. The warm climate of Florida attracts many winter tourists.

16. That movie has been shown on television many times.

17. Acres of wheat rippled in the breeze.

18. That mechanic completed the job in record time.

19. The people in that picture were boarding a plane for London.

20. One can find rocks of fantastic shapes in the Garden of the Gods, near Colorado Springs.

21. The city of Albuquerque is five thousand feet above sea level.

22. The apple trees have fragrant blossoms.

23. Sequoias, the world's tallest trees, are found in California.

24. John Banister was an early Virginia botanist.

25. The tall pine trees hide our tiny cabin.

26. The lady filled the vase with colorful flowers.

Simple Subjects and Predicates, p. 2

 Draw a line between the complete subject and the complete predicate in each sentence. Underline the simple subject once and the simple predicate twice.

27. A sudden clap of thunder frightened all of us.

28. The soft snow covered the fields and roads.

29. We drove very slowly over the narrow bridge.

30. Suzanne's friend got a job at the aquarium.

31. Our class read about the founder of Hull House.

32. Maria's little boys were playing in the park near her house.

33. This album has many folk songs.

34. We are making the sandwiches for our office party.

35. All of the trees on that lawn are giant oaks.

36. Many Americans are working in foreign countries.

37. The manager read the names of the contest winners.

38. Jerome brought these large melons.

39. We opened the front door of the house.

40. The two mechanics worked on the car for an hour.

41. Black and yellow butterflies fluttered among the flowers.

42. The little girl spoke politely.

43. We found many beautiful shells along the shore.

44. The best part of the program is the dance number.

45. Every ambitious person is working hard.

46. Sheryl swam across the lake two times.

47. Our program will begin at eight o'clock.

48. The handle of this basket is different.

49. The clock in the tower strikes every hour.

50. The white farmhouse on that road belongs to my cousin.

51. The first game of the season will be played tomorrow.

52. The plants sprouted quickly after the first rain.

53. The television program was very helpful.

54. I used a word processor to write the paper.

55. My brother's truck is in the driveway.

 Write two sentences about yourself. Draw a line between the complete subject and the complete predicate. Underline the simple subject once and the simple predicate twice.

56. _____

57. _____

Compound Subjects

> • A **compound subject** is made up of two or more simple subjects.
>   EXAMPLE: **LaRon** and **Katherine** are tall people.

✳ **Draw a line between the complete subject and the complete predicate in each sentence. Write SS for a simple subject. Write CS for a compound subject.**

_____ 1. Arturo and I often work late on Friday.

_____ 2. Sandy left the person near the crowded exit.

_____ 3. She and I will mail the packages to San Francisco today.

_____ 4. Detroit and Chicago are two frequently visited cities.

_____ 5. The fire spread rapidly to other buildings in the neighborhood.

_____ 6. Luis and Tara helped their children with their homework.

_____ 7. Swimming, jogging, and hiking were our favorite sports.

_____ 8. Melbourne and Sydney are important Australian cities.

_____ 9. Eric and I had an interesting experience Saturday.

_____ 10. The Red Sea and the Mediterranean Sea are connected by the Suez Canal.

_____ 11. The Astros and the Angels are two baseball teams.

_____ 12. The people waved to us from the top of the cliff.

_____ 13. Hiroshi and Ron helped us move to our new apartment.

_____ 14. Clean clothes and a neat appearance are important in an interview.

_____ 15. Raymond's son and his faithful dog are never far apart.

_____ 16. Dave and Pablo are on their way to the swimming pool.

_____ 17. Thomas combed his daughter's shiny black hair.

_____ 18. Redbud and dogwood trees bloom in the spring.

_____ 19. I hummed a cheerful tune on the way to the meeting.

_____ 20. Buffalo, deer, and antelope roamed the plains.

_____ 21. Livia and her sister are very talented singers.

_____ 22. Vancouver and Calgary are two cities in Canada.

_____ 23. Hang gliding is a popular sport in Hawaii.

_____ 24. Our neighbors asked us to come for dinner on Tuesday.

_____ 25. The doctor asked him to get a blood test.

✳ **Write two sentences with compound subjects.**

26. _____

27. _____

Language: Usage and Practice HS, SV 1419027867

Name _____   Date _____

Compound Predicates

> • A **compound predicate** is made up of two or more simple predicates.
>   EXAMPLE: Esther / **dances** and **sings**.

Draw a line between the complete subject and the complete predicate in each sentence. Write <u>SP</u> for each simple predicate. Write <u>CP</u> for each compound predicate.

_____ 1. Jarrell grinned and nodded.

_____ 2. Plants need air to live.

_____ 3. Old silver tea kettles were among their possessions.

_____ 4. My aunt buys and sells real estate.

_____ 5. Snow covered every highway in the county.

_____ 6. Mr. Sander designs and makes odd pieces of furniture.

_____ 7. Popcorn is one of my favorite snack foods.

_____ 8. Aerobic dancing is a good way to stay fit.

_____ 9. The ducks crossed the road and found the ducklings.

_____ 10. They came early and stayed late.

_____ 11. Crystal participated in the Special Olympics this year.

_____ 12. Marci raked and sacked the leaves.

_____ 13. Perry built the fire and cooked supper.

_____ 14. We collected old newspapers for the recycling center.

_____ 15. Daniel arrived in Cincinnati during the afternoon.

_____ 16. Jenny's parents are visiting in Oregon and Washington.

_____ 17. The Garzas live in that apartment building on Oak Street.

_____ 18. Alex and his crew picked up and delivered the shingles today.

_____ 19. The audience talked and laughed before the performance.

_____ 20. Automobiles crowd and jam that highway early in the morning.

_____ 21. The apples are rotting in the boxes.

_____ 22. The leader of the group grumbled and scolded.

_____ 23. She worked hard and waited patiently.

_____ 24. Benjamin Franklin was a great American.

_____ 25. The supervisor has completed the work for the week.

Write two sentences with compound predicates.

26. _____

27. _____

Unit 2: Sentences
Language: Usage and Practice HS, SV 1419027867

Position of Subjects

- When the subject of a sentence comes before the verb, the sentence is in **natural order**.
    - EXAMPLE: Travis <u>went</u> to the park.
- When the verb or part of the verb comes before the subject, the sentence is in **inverted order**.
    - EXAMPLES: Here <u>are</u> the <u>calculators</u>.
    - Down <u>came</u> the <u>rain</u>.
- A question may be written in inverted order.
    - EXAMPLE: Where <u>is</u> the <u>restaurant</u>?
- In a command or request, the subject of the sentence may not be expressed. The understood subject is <u>you</u>.
    - EXAMPLE: <u>Call</u> about the job now.
    - (You) <u>call</u> about the job now.

 Rewrite each inverted sentence in natural order. Underline the simple subject once and the simple predicate twice. Add <u>you</u> as the subject to commands or requests.

1. When is the movie playing?

The <u>movie</u> is <u>playing</u> when?

_____

2. Never will I forget my first train trip.

_____

3. Here is the best picture in the poster shop.

_____

4. Seldom has he been ill.

_____

5. Out went the lights.

_____

6. There were bookcases on all sides of the room.

_____

7. Around the sharp curve swerved the speeding car.

_____

8. Get out of the swimming pool during the thunderstorm.

_____

9. There are still two children in the pool.

_____

　Language: Usage and Practice HS, SV 1419027867

Name _____   Date _____

Simple and Compound Sentences

- A **simple sentence** has one subject and one predicate.
  - EXAMPLE: Earth / is covered by land and water.
- A **compound sentence** is made up of two simple sentences joined by a connecting word such as <u>and</u>, <u>but</u>, and <u>or</u>. A comma comes before the connecting word.
  - EXAMPLE: One-fourth of Earth / is covered by land, **and** the land / is divided into seven continents.

 Draw a line between each complete subject and complete predicate. Before each sentence, write <u>S</u> for simple sentence or <u>C</u> for compound sentence.

_____S_____ **1.** The seven continents of the world / are North America, South America, Africa, Europe, Australia, Asia, and Antarctica.

_____ **2.** Three-fourths of Earth is covered by water, and most of it is salty ocean water.

_____ **3.** The four oceans of the world are the Pacific, the Atlantic, the Indian, and the Arctic.

_____ **4.** We cannot exist without water, but we cannot drink the salty ocean water.

_____ **5.** Most of our drinking water comes from lakes, rivers, and streams.

_____ **6.** Clean water is a priceless resource.

 Combine each pair of simple sentences below into a compound sentence.

7. The Pacific Ocean is the world's largest ocean.
It covers more area than all the land put together.

_____

_____

8. Smaller bodies of salt water are called seas, gulfs, or bays.
They are often encircled by land.

_____

_____

9. Seas, gulfs, and bays are joined to the oceans.
They vary in size and depth.

_____

_____

10. You could spend your vacation at the Mediterranean.
You could spend your vacation touring Asia.

_____

_____

Unit 2: Sentences
Language: Usage and Practice HS, SV 1419027867

Run-on Sentences

- When two sentences run together without punctuation or with only a comma to separate them, a **run-on sentence** results.
- Run-on sentences occur because of punctuation errors.
  - EXAMPLE: **run-on sentence:**
    - I have to take the cat to the vet then I have to go to the mall.
  - **correct sentence:**
    - After I take the cat to the vet, I have to go to the mall.
  - **correct sentence:**
    - I have to take the cat to the vet; then I have to go to the mall.
  - **correct sentence:**
    - I have to take the cat to the vet, and then I have to go to the mall.
  - **two correct sentences:**
    - I have to take the cat to the vet. Then I have to go to the mall.

Read the sentences below. Write R if the sentence is a run-on sentence and C if the sentence is a correct sentence.

_____ 1. Marcia learns so many things each summer when she works at a community day camp, being with children always makes her happy.

_____ 2. Her favorite sport is soccer, but she especially enjoys teaching young children to play basketball.

_____ 3. Marcia supervises twelve children she often plays "getting-to-know-you" games to learn about each child.

_____ 4. Her friends Fernando and Anna also work in the program, the three of them often combine their groups to do activities together.

_____ 5. When a child is homesick, Marcia comforts him or her.

_____ 6. Elena, the swim instructor, teaches children who can't swim at all, she also helps those who can swim to improve their skills.

_____ 7. Mr. Sung is in charge of the day camp he's like a father to the children.

_____ 8. In order to work at the day camp, you must be at least eighteen years old.

_____ 9. Arts and crafts activities are very popular; however, sports are the most popular activities.

_____ 10. The children have lunch and take a nap each day.

_____ 11. Marcia hopes she can work there next summer, but she knows many other people who would like to have her job.

_____ 12. Mr. Sung will give her a good recommendation, he likes her and thinks she does a good job.

_____ 13. I like to watch old movies, and The Wizard of Oz is one of my favorites.

_____ 14. Use machine oil to lubricate the chain of your bicycle if you do, it will last longer.

_____ 15. Have you ever seen a meteor fall from the sky they turn to dust before they hit Earth?

Language: Usage and Practice HS, SV 1419027867

Run-on Sentences, p. 2

> • Run-on sentences can be corrected in several ways.
> • Run-on sentences can be corrected by making a compound sentence with a comma and a coordinate conjunction (<u>and</u>, <u>but</u>, <u>or</u>, <u>nor</u>, <u>for</u>, <u>so</u>).
>> EXAMPLE: **run-on sentence:**
>>> We heard the siren, it was barely loud enough to notice.
>> **compound sentence:**
>>> We heard the siren, but it was barely loud enough to notice.
> • Run-on sentences can be corrected by making a compound sentence with a semicolon to link the sentences.
>> EXAMPLE: **compound sentence:**
>>> We heard the siren; it was barely loud enough to notice.
> • Run-on sentences can be corrected by making two simple sentences.
>> EXAMPLE: **two simple sentences:**
>>> We heard the siren. It was barely loud enough to notice.

 Write each run-on sentence correctly.

16. A lot of coffee is grown in South America, the mild climate is ideal for coffee plantations.

A lot of coffee is grown in South America, for the mild climate is ideal for coffee plantations.

_____

17. Mr. and Mrs. Owens took their family to the beach for the Fourth of July fireworks display, it has become so crowded there they'd rather take them somewhere else.

_____

_____

18. Ask her again tell her you didn't hear the question.

_____

_____

19. Regina isn't working this shift, she is working the next shift.

_____

_____

20. I'm going to the supermarket first, I'm going to the drugstore next.

_____

_____

21. The tide was rising quickly, everyone got out of the water.

_____

_____

 First, write a run-on sentence. Then correct it in three different ways: use a comma and conjunction, use a semicolon, and make two separate sentences. Use your own paper.

Language: Usage and Practice HS, SV 1419027867

Unit 2 Test

Label each sentence or group of words. Before each sentence, write D for declarative, IN for interrogative, IM for imperative, or E for exclamatory. Put the correct punctuation at the end. Before each group of words that is not a sentence, write F for fragment.

_____ 1. WXYZ is my favorite radio station____

_____ 2. This week it is having a contest____

_____ 3. Call the station to win a prize____

_____ 4. If you are the seventh caller____

_____ 5. The winner will be announced immediately____

_____ 6. I just won____

_____ 7. What is the prize____

_____ 8. A trip to the Super Bowl____

_____ 9. That is terrific____

Rewrite each fragment to make it a complete sentence.

10. Needed to buy a gallon of milk.

_____

11. Because the store was closed when he got there.

_____

_____

12. Drove around lost for over an hour.

_____

13. The problem being he did not know where he was going.

_____

_____

Draw a line between the complete subject and the complete predicate in each sentence. Underline the simple subject once and the simple predicate twice.

14. You must guess the number of beans in the jar.

15. Jon will write his guesses on these pieces of paper.

16. On the counter can be found pencils.

17. Melinda has already written her guess.

18. They are eager to find the answer.

19. Jon is the winner.

One of the sentences above is in inverted order. Rewrite it in natural order.

20. _____

Name _____   Date _____

Unit 2 Test, p. 2

Before each sentence, write CS for compound subject, CP for compound predicate, or C for compound sentence.

_____ 21. Contestants buy something and fill out a form.

_____ 22. Rules and dates for a contest are often printed on the entry form.

_____ 23. I think of contests as challenging, and I often enter them.

_____ 24. I enjoy the suspense of a contest and look forward to the results.

_____ 25. Jake and I are going to buy a blender.

_____ 26. We will go to the store and choose the one we want.

_____ 27. I like shopping, and Jake likes to go with me.

_____ 28. I prefer the big mall, but Jake likes the smaller one.

_____ 29. He and I will also do our Christmas shopping then.

Some of the following groups of words are run-on sentences. Other groups are correct sentences. Write RO before each run-on sentence.

_____ 30. I can't believe that he would allow that to happen.

_____ 31. What does that matter I suppose being right is the only thing that matters?

_____ 32. He won't accept how many people have refused to sign the petition.

_____ 33. Then he is being silly people can do whatever they want to do.

_____ 34. I have an idea why not make a petition that he will not sign.

_____ 35. Religion and politics are always touchy subjects.

Rewrite each run-on sentence to make it correct.

36. Games have been around for thousands of years in Egypt alone at least four games were played as early as 2700 B.C.

_____

_____

37. New games are being created all the time only some will stand the test of time.

_____

_____

38. I have an idea for a new game would you like to play it?

_____

_____

Language: Usage and Practice HS, SV 1419027867

Name _____   Date _____

Nouns

> • A **noun** is a word that names a person, place, thing, or quality.
>   EXAMPLE: **Nick Nately** is my oldest **friend.**

 Circle the nouns in each sentence.

1. (Lupe Garza) has worked here for (years) and is now a (supervisor)

2. The piece of land shaped like a triangle at the mouth of a river is called a delta.

3. Gilbert Stuart painted the portraits of five presidents of the United States.

4. Albert Einstein, one of the greatest scientists in history, was born in Germany.

5. The greatest library of the ancient world was in Alexandria, Egypt.

6, Jim Thorpe, a Sac Indian, is ranked among the greatest athletes in the world.

7. Mahalia Jackson was noted as a singer of religious folk songs called spirituals.

8. Marconi invented the wireless telegraph.

9. Do you watch the parades and football on television on New Year's Day?

10. Pocahontas, daughter of Powhatan, saved the life of Captain John Smith.

11. The *Boston News-Letter* was the first newspaper in the United States.

12. The first wireless message was sent across the English Channel in the nineteenth century.

13. Chicago is a city on Lake Michigan.

14. Our house is on a nice street with many trees.

15. Mei likes her new job at Shoppers World.

16. Have you ever traveled to Nova Scotia or Prince Edward Island?

17. Washington, D.C., is the capital of the United States.

18. Potatoes and apples are important crops in some provinces of Canada.

19. Jessica was excited about her new car.

20. Hailstones are frozen raindrops, but snowflakes are not.

21. The days are usually warm in the summer.

22. Many rivers in North America were named by explorers.

23. Trey built new bookshelves for his apartment.

24. California is home to many stars from the movies.

25. William Caxton printed the first book in England.

26. Christi bought tomatoes, lettuce, and cherries at the market.

27. That building has offices, stores, and apartments.

28. Marcy drove to Peoria to see her daughter.

29. The airport was closed for five hours because of a snowstorm.

30. My pen is almost out of ink.

Name _____   Date _____

Common and Proper Nouns

- There are two main classes of **nouns**: common and proper nouns.
- A **common noun** names any one of a class of objects.
    EXAMPLES: man, town, flower
- A **proper noun** names a particular person, place, or thing. It begins with a capital letter.
    EXAMPLES: Miss Paxtel, Miami, Hoover Dam

 Underline each common noun.

1. The sturdy timber of the oak is used to construct furniture, bridges, and ships.

2. Robert Fulton was a painter, jeweler, farmer, engineer, and inventor.

3. The main crops of Puerto Rico are sugar, tobacco, coffee, and fruits.

4. The groves of Texas provide enough pecans for the eastern part of the United States.

5. Michigan has many rivers, waterfalls, and lakes.

6. The Verrazano-Narrows Bridge between Brooklyn and Staten Island is the longest bridge of its kind in the world.

7. Some of the main foods eaten in Greece are lamb, fish, olives, and cheese.

8. A road passes through a tunnel cut in the base of a giant tree in California.

9. Since the earliest civilizations, gold has been used for ornaments.

10. Among the largest lakes in North America is Lake Erie.

11. A tree bearing beautiful blossoms and delicious fruit is the orange.

12. Rockefeller Center is a large center of entertainment in New York City.

 Underline each proper noun.

13. Some principal crops grown in the United States are apples, corn, cotton, oats, potatoes, and wheat.

14. William Penn was the founder of Pennsylvania.

15. The Elm Grove Library has five copies of the book by Amy Tan.

16. Commander Byrd, a naval officer, made the first flight to the North Pole.

17. Dr. Jeanne Spurlock went to Howard University College of Medicine.

18. Oranges were brought to Europe from Asia.

19. Colombia is the world's leading producer of emeralds.

20. Mount Kilimanjaro is the tallest mountain in Africa.

21. The Navajo Indians make beautiful silver and turquoise jewelry.

22. Leticia and Carlos anchored the tent while Samantha and Ted prepared the food.

23. Thomas Jefferson introduced the system of coinage used in the United States.

24. Their home is on the shore of Lake Michigan.

25. Quebec is the only walled city in North America.

Language: Usage and Practice HS, SV 1419027867

Singular and Plural Nouns

The following chart shows how to change **singular nouns** into **plural nouns**.

Noun	Plural Form	Examples
Most nouns	Add <u>s</u>	ship, ships nose, noses
Nouns ending in a consonant and <u>y</u>	Change the <u>y</u> to <u>i</u> and add <u>es</u>	sky, skies navy, navies
Nouns ending in <u>o</u>	Add <u>s</u> or <u>es</u>	hero, heroes video, videos
Most nouns ending in <u>f</u> or <u>fe</u>	Change the <u>f</u> or <u>fe</u> to <u>ves</u>	half, halves knife, knives
Most nouns ending in <u>ch</u>, <u>sh</u>, <u>s</u>, or <u>x</u>	Add <u>es</u>	inch, inches dish, dishes mess, messes tax, taxes
Many two-word or three-word compound nouns	Add <u>s</u> to the principal word	son-in-law, sons-in-law
Nouns with the same form in the singular and plural	No change	sheep deer trout fish
Nouns with no singular form	No change	scissors slacks mumps pants
Nouns with irregular plurals	Change the entire word	foot, feet child, children
Figures, symbols, signs, letters, and words considered as words	Add an apostrophe and <u>s</u>	m, m's 5, 5's +, +'s and, and's

 Write the plural for each singular noun.

1. county _____

2. waltz _____

3. tomato _____

4. mouse _____

5. match _____

6. calf _____

7. century _____

8. trench _____

9. bookcase _____

10. piano _____

11. desk _____

12. goose _____

13. radio _____

14. fly _____

15. child _____

16. dress _____

Name _____ Date _____

Singular and Plural Nouns, p. 2

 Complete each sentence with the plural form of the word in parentheses.

17. (brush) These are plastic _____.

18. (lunch) That cafe on the corner serves well-balanced _____.

19. (country) Which _____ belong to the United Nations?

20. (bench) There are many iron _____ in the park.

21. (earring) These _____ came from Italy.

22. (county) How many _____ are in that state?

23. (piano) There are three _____ in the warehouse.

24. (fox) Did you see the _____ at the zoo?

25. (checkers) Mr. Murphy enjoys playing _____ with his grandchild.

26. (potato) Do you like baked _____?

27. (dish) Please help wash the _____.

28. (store) There are three _____ near my house.

29. (penny) How many _____ make a dollar?

30. (dress) Mandy makes all of her own _____.

31. (bridge) How many _____ were destroyed by the flood?

32. (city) Can you name the four largest _____ in your state?

33. (deer) The photographers brought back photos of three _____.

34. (flash) The vivid _____ of lightning frightened everyone.

35. (coach) That football team employs five _____.

36. (e) How many _____ are in the word Tennessee?

37. (mouse) We found a nest of _____ in the field by our house.

38. (box) We need several more _____ to pack for our move.

39. (scarf) Dale gave me three _____.

40. (n) Rickie makes her _____ too much like u's.

41. (radio) Kirk has a large collection of old _____ he keeps on display.

42. (90) Miss Smithers gave three _____ on the math test.

43. (woman) A dozen _____ attended the conference.

Unit 3: Grammar and Usage
Language: Usage and Practice HS, SV 1419027867

Possessive Nouns

- A **possessive noun** shows possession of the noun that follows.
    - EXAMPLES: **Gary's** football   **Shonna's** gloves
- Form the possessive of most singular nouns by adding an **apostrophe** (')
  and s.
    - EXAMPLES: **Josie's** pillow   **Sandy's** eyes
- Form the possessive of most plural nouns ending in s by adding only an
  apostrophe.
    - EXAMPLES: **birds'** nests   **lions'** dens
- Form the possessive of plural nouns that do not end in s by adding an
  apostrophe and s.
    - EXAMPLE: **men's** suits

 Underline the possessive nouns in each sentence.

1. Steve's glasses are on my desk.

2. Mary is wearing her mother's gold bracelet.

3. My sister's team has chosen her as their best player.

4. The speaker's first statement caused us to change our minds.

5. We have formed a collectors' group.

6. Rosie's husband found the child's lost puppy.

7. The Tarrens' store was damaged by the recent storm.

8. What are the president's duties?

9. When does the new mayor's term of office begin?

10. Leslie, Anthony's notebook is on your desk.

11. We went to the women's department.

12. The family's income was reduced.

13. Our day's work is done.

14. The lifeguard's heroism was rewarded.

15. Our store's holiday sale was a great success.

16. Has Ms. Herrera opened a children's store?

17. Harry's cooking is improving.

18. We borrowed Jim's hammer.

19. May I see Darrell's picture?

20. I'll meet you at the Lees' house.

21. Lucia visited Mark's college.

22. Frank's telephone call was about Alex's accident.

23. Mr. Randolph stood at his neighbors' gate.

24. Is that the Kashons' parking place?

25. Canada's flag has a red maple leaf.

Name _____ Date _____

Possessive Nouns, p. 2

 Write the possessive form of each noun.

26. girl _____

27. child _____

28. women _____

29. children _____

30. Jason _____

31. Julia _____

32. students _____

33. father _____

34. babies _____

35. dog _____

36. baby _____

37. boys _____

38. teacher _____

39. Dr. Kay _____

40. ladies _____

41. table _____

42. mothers _____

43. players _____

44. nieces _____

45. club _____

46. brother _____

47. soldier _____

48. men _____

49. aunt _____

50. writers _____

51. waiter _____

52. driver _____

53. bird _____

54. actors _____

55. cats _____

 Rewrite each phrase by using a possessive noun.

56. the cap belonging to Rick _____

57. the wrench that belongs to Katy _____

58. the cry of the baby _____

59. the house that my cousins own _____

60. the new shoes that belong to Kim _____

61. the collar of the dog _____

62. the books that Enrique owns _____

63. the office of the superintendent _____

64. the friends of our neighbors _____

65. the opinion of the editor _____

66. the lunches of the children _____

67. the coat belonging to Mei Ling _____

68. the assignment of the teacher _____

69. the babysitter of the boy _____

70. the keys belonging to the manager _____

Unit 3: Grammar and Usage
Language: Usage and Practice HS, SV 1419027867

Count and Noncount Nouns

- A **count noun** names a person, place, thing, or quality that can be counted. A count noun has both singular and plural forms.
  - EXAMPLE: one **student**   two **students**
- A **noncount noun** names a person, place, thing, or quality that cannot be counted. A noncount noun does not have a plural form.
  - EXAMPLES: **money**   **health**   **time**
- Some words can be used only with plural count nouns: <u>these</u>, <u>those</u>, <u>few</u>, <u>fewer</u>, <u>many</u>, <u>several</u>, <u>a number of</u>.
  - EXAMPLES: **few** students   **those** footballs   **a number of** chances
- Some words can be used only with noncount nouns: <u>less</u>, <u>little</u>, <u>much</u>, <u>a great deal of</u>.
  - EXAMPLES: **much** money   **little** time   **a great deal of** fun
- <u>This</u> and <u>that</u> can be used with both noncount nouns and singular count nouns. <u>A lot of</u> can be used with both noncount nouns and plural count nouns.
  - EXAMPLES: **this** friend   **that** music   **a lot of** friends   **a lot of** music

---

 Underline the correct word or words in parentheses to complete each sentence.

1. (fewer, less)   Please try to make _____ mistakes.

2. (this, those)   I will take _____ money to the bank.

3. (few, little)   Armando offered _____ help when we needed it.

4. (less, few)   Nekeshia likes food with _____ calories and a lot of taste.

5. (a great deal of, a number of)   My brother has _____ friends.

6. (many, much)   Will _____ people fit around this table?

7. (a little, a few)   All I need from Arleen is _____ advice.

8. (many, much)   The greeting card wished us _____ happiness.

9. (less, fewer)   Jonna has _____ time to see us since she had the baby.

10. (a lot of, a number of)   The bowl held _____ cereal.

11. (a little, a few)   I have _____ minutes left until work is over.

12. (that, those)   Do you like _____ set of dishes?

13. (a great deal of, a number of)   Julian has _____ questions about the schedule.

14. (a great deal of, a number of)   Kimberly swept _____ dust into the hall.

15. (several, much)   Angela wore _____ rings on her left hand.

16. (a number of, a lot of)   She has _____ jewelry to choose from.

17. (a little, a few)   She also wore _____ silver bracelets.

18. (fewer, less)   Tamara has _____ friends since she moved.

19. (little, few)   She has _____ time to meet new people.

Verbs

> • A **verb** is a word that expresses action or state of being.
>   EXAMPLES:
>   Chelsea **went** to school.
>   These books **are** yours.
>   Lizabeth and Patrick **sing** in the school choir.

 Underline the verb in each sentence.

  1. Where are the Rocky Mountains?

  2. W. C. Handy wrote "Saint Louis Blues."

  3. Check your papers carefully.

  4. Bananas have great food value.

  5. Africa is the home of the hippopotamus.

  6. The car reached the narrow bridge.

  7. Gwendolyn Brooks won a Pulitzer Prize.

  8. Ricardo trains good mechanics.

  9. Felicia wears a black wool coat to the office.

 10. How many stars are on the U.S. flag?

 11. The people of our town remember the cold winter.

 12. Peter Minuit bought Manhattan for about twenty-four dollars.

 13. What is your favorite book?

 14. They followed the old trail to the top of the hill.

 15. The wind whistled around the corner.

 16. Ericka always watches the news.

 17. Their team scored twice in the first half.

 18. Which driver won the car race?

 19. The big house on the corner is white.

 20. Mexico is the southern neighbor of the United States.

 21. Taylor set the table for five people.

 22. Answer my question.

 23. Mrs. Sung explained the commands on the computer for us.

 24. Rashid worked in an electronics assembly plant.

 25. Our town has a public swimming pool.

 26. My son plays the saxophone in the band.

 27. Brush your teeth frequently.

 28. A puff of wind whirled the leaves over the lawn.

 29. We arrived at our camp early in the morning.

 30. Where is the launching pad?

Action Verbs

> • An **action verb** is a verb that expresses action.
>   EXAMPLE: The track star **ran** fast.

 Underline the action verb in each sentence.

1. Watch your favorite television program.
2. Andrea carefully dusted her new piano.
3. Anna, copy the addresses correctly.
4. A wood fire burned in the huge fireplace.
5. This button fell off my favorite sweater.
6. The Harlem Globetrotters play basketball throughout the world.
7. The musicians practiced for the concert.
8. The waves dashed the small boat against the rocks.
9. A sentence expresses a complete thought.
10. Everybody enjoys a good laugh.
11. This long, narrow trail leads to the mountaintop.
12. It snowed almost every day in February.
13. We hiked through the southern part of Arizona.
14. Dan made me a delicious sandwich.
15. Please hand me the salt, Mom.
16. Draw a line under each verb.
17. We skated on Lake Superior.
18. The tour guide answered all my questions.
19. The city repaired that pothole last week.
20. Early settlers suffered many hardships in their travels.
21. Address your application letter to the personnel director.
22. They moved the car from the street.
23. Thomas Edison often worked eighteen hours a day.
24. Carlo directs the community choir.
25. The team played soccer all afternoon.
26. We walked along the beach for an hour.
27. Who helped you with your science project?
28. The old bridge collapsed.
29. The antique clock ticked loudly.
30. Ava ate everything on her plate.
31. Bernard cheered for his son's team.

48

Name _____ Date _____

Linking Verbs

- A **linking verb** does not show action. Instead, it links the subject to a word that describes or identifies the subject.
- Verbs that show state of being are linking verbs (am, is, are, was, were).
    - EXAMPLES:
        - We **were** cold.
        - Jancy **is** a dancer.
- A verb is a linking verb if it can replace one of the verbs of being (for example: look, feel, taste, smell, sound, seem, become).
    - EXAMPLES:
        - Jarret **looked** tired.
        - The soup **tastes** delicious.

 Underline the linking verb in each sentence.

1. Karla appears nervous.
2. She is the first singer on the program.
3. Last year she was last on the program.
4. Another performer is last this year.
5. The stage looks beautiful.
6. The bouquets are gifts from friends.
7. The flowers smell fresh.
8. Karla feels ready to start.
9. Her song sounds wonderful.
10. The audience seems pleased.

11. Jacob is a dancer and Karla's partner.
12. He feels confident about his performance.
13. He is ready to go onstage.
14. A week ago he was worried about this event.
15. Now he is certain about all his dance moves.
16. Karla looks proud as she watches Jacob.
17. Karla and Jacob are happy about the show.
18. The audience seems thrilled.
19. Afterward, all of the food tastes delicious.
20. Jacob and Karla are excited.

 Complete each sentence with a linking verb from the box. You may use the verbs more than once.

am	appeared	are	became	is	seemed	was	were

21. Toby _____ frightened.

22. He _____ alone in the cabin for the first time.

23. In the dark forest, everything _____ threatening.

24. Because of the storm, the lights _____ dim.

25. Even the shadows _____ strange.

26. "This _____ stupid," he thought to himself.

27. "I _____ brave; I'm not a coward."

28. "Where _____ Pablo?" he wondered.

29. "There _____ bears in the woods."

30. "What if Pablo _____ lost?" Toby worried.

Name _____ Date _____

Verb Phrases

> • A sentence may contain a **verb phrase**. A verb phrase is a main verb with one or more helping verbs.
>
> EXAMPLES:
> The girls **are singing**.
> Where **have** you **been**?

 Underline the verb or verb phrase in each sentence.

1. The first schools were held in homes.

2. Who invented the jet engine?

3. The *New England Primer* was the earliest textbook in the United States.

4. John Philip Sousa was a bandmaster and composer.

5. Who built the first motorcycle?

6. My friends will arrive on Saturday afternoon.

7. What was the final score?

8. Ryan has made this unusual birdhouse.

9. The waves covered the beach with many shells.

10. I have ridden on a motor scooter.

11. The artist is molding clay.

12. Belle and her family spent last summer in the Ozarks.

13. The supervisor posted the names of the new employees.

14. Aaron has found a new hat.

15. She is going to the store.

16. We have trimmed the hedges.

17. Our nation exports many kinds of food.

18. My friend is reading a book about World War II.

19. Jane Addams helped many foreign-born people in Chicago.

20. Oil was discovered in West Texas.

21. Jenny Lind was called "the Swedish Nightingale."

22. We are planning a car trip to Kansas City.

23. That dog has howled for two hours.

24. Our guests have arrived.

25. I have written letters to several companies.

26. I can name three important cities in this state.

27. The hummingbird received its name because of the sound of its wings.

28. Jolene's poem was in the newspaper.

29. Chuck and Patty are working at the hamburger stand.

30. Before the flood, we had painted the house dark green.

Name _____   Date _____

Helping Vers

- The last word of a verb phrase is the **main verb**.
- The other words in a verb phrase are **helping verbs**.

                helping verb   main verb

  EXAMPLES: ↓   ↓

      Angie and Jon **were** **playing** in their yard.

      The manager   **had**   **displayed** the apples.

- The helping verbs are:

      am, are, is, was, were, be, being, been **(forms of be)**

      have, has, had **(forms of have)**

      do, does, did **(forms of do)**

      can, could, shall, should, will, would, must, may, might

 Underline the verb phrase and circle the helping verb in each sentence below.

1. Mina and Mick have begun their spring cleaning.

2. Mina will rake the leaves on the front lawn.

3. Mick must clean the garage.

4. Together they will wash all the windows.

5. Some friends might prepare lunch for the two of them.

6. The cooks should wash their hands first.

7. Sandwiches and fruit salad would make a delicious lunch on a hot day.

8. Their next-door neighbor is working on his lawn, too.

9. He has sprayed his front and back lawns with a fertilizer.

10. Every worker must close the garbage bags tightly.

11. Squirrels, raccoons, and large crows would enjoy the garbage.

12. They might finish the outside work today.

13. You must arrive here by tomorrow.

14. Did anyone like the movie?

15. The painters may paint the side of the house.

16. Jennifer is visiting her sister in Vancouver.

17. The musician had practiced the piece several times.

18. Who will drive us to the hospital?

19. The actor has read the script.

20. Jerome and his co-workers were playing baseball in the field.

21. The schoolchildren had begun their homework.

22. She will drive to Cleveland.

23. I will eat my lunch soon.

24. Do you want this brown coat?

25. We shall enter the contest tomorrow.

Helping Verbs, p. 2

- A verb phrase may have more than one helping verb.

  EXAMPLES:
         helping verb   main verb

  Bill **should have** **taken** the bus to school.
  My plants **have been** **growing** very quickly.

- In a question or in a sentence with a word such as <u>not</u> or <u>never</u>, the helping verb may be separated from the main verb.

  EXAMPLES:
  When **will** you **decide** about your bicycle?
  Jason **has** not **fixed** his bicycle.

 Underline the verb phrases and circle the helping verbs.

26. Our final exam (will be) given on May 10.

27. Many students have been studying every night.

28. My friends and I may be forming a study group.

29. The study group members should be reviewing each chapter.

30. Are you joining our study group?

31. May we meet in your house one afternoon next week?

32. Kim, Jim, and Tim should have known the answers to the first ten questions.

33. Where have you been all day?

34. I have been looking everywhere for you.

35. I would have met you earlier.

36. The flight has been delayed in Atlanta.

37. Would you prefer an earlier flight?

38. I had been enjoying a long visit with my parents.

39. My sister has been waiting for more than two hours.

40. Lois and Jeremy had been at the pool all day.

41. Will any other adults be swimming in the pool?

42. Several neighborhood children must have been splashing each other.

43. Can Jessica and Maria take lessons next summer?

44. We have not signed them up for lessons before.

45. But they have been practicing every day.

46. Will you tell me about these lessons?

47. Has Brandon seen Jesse's new sneakers?

48. Brandon had been wanting a pair just like Jesse's.

49. However, he will not be upset about it.

50. Brandon will never buy such a costly pair of shoes.

51. Reggie has been hitting tennis balls every day at noon.

52. He has not eaten during his lunchtime.

Name _____ Date _____

Subject-Verb Agreement

- A **singular subject** must have a **singular verb**.
    EXAMPLES:
        Janet **lives** there.
        Does she **walk** to work?
        She **doesn't live** near the bus.
- A **plural subject** must have a **plural verb**.
    EXAMPLES:
        Janet and her sister **live** there.
        Do they **walk** to work?
        They **don't live** near the bus.
- You and I must have plural verbs.

 Underline the subject of each sentence. Write <u>S</u> above each singular subject and <u>P</u> above each plural subject. Then underline the correct verb form in parentheses to complete the sentence.

1. Many stories (tell, tells) how dogs become friends of people.

2. A story by Rudyard Kipling (say, says) that Wild Dog agrees to help hunt and guard in exchange for bones.

3. After that, Wild Dog (become, becomes) First Friend.

4. Many dogs never (leave, leaves) their masters.

5. In another story of loyalty in the wild, an Arctic dog (doesn't, don't) leave his master's dead body.

6. There are few people in history that (hasn't, haven't) recorded the usefulness of dogs.

7. Studies in Egypt (prove, proves) that the dog was a companion in ancient Egypt.

8. Bones of dogs (has, have) appeared in Egyptian graves.

9. Ancient Greek vases (picture, pictures) dogs on them.

10. Today the Leader Dog organization (train, trains) dogs to guide the blind.

11. One blind man said, "My eyes (have, has) a wet nose."

12. A dog (does, do) have excellent hearing and smelling abilities.

13. What society (doesn't, don't) agree that a dog is a person's best friend?

14. Dogs (is, are) very loyal and devoted.

15. Sometimes a dog (need, needs) to go to obedience school.

16. Dogs (find, finds) out how to obey their masters there.

17. Many people (agree, agrees) that a trained dog is wonderful company.

18. A dog (doesn't, don't) always want just dog food.

19. Dogs also (likes, like) to eat dinner scraps!

Name _____ Date _____

Verb Tenses

- The **tense** of a verb tells the time: present, past, or future.
- **Present tense** means that something happens in the present.
  - EXAMPLES:
    - Mandy **dances** in the show.
    - My piano lessons **start** today.
- **Past tense** means that something happened in the past. Regular past tense verbs end in d or ed.
  - EXAMPLES:
    - Mandy **danced** in the show.
    - My piano lessons **started** last June.
- **Future tense** means that something will happen in the future. Future tense verbs use will.
  - EXAMPLES:
    - Mandy **will dance** in the show.
    - My piano lessons **will start** next month.

 Write present, past, or future for the tense of each underlined verb.

1. My computer class will end next week. _____future_____

2. I really learned a lot. _____

3. I never worked with computers before. _____

4. I dream of a computer of my own now. _____

5. My new job will start soon. _____

6. I need computer skills for the job. _____

7. I signed up for the class to learn about them. _____

8. The job will use all my new skills. _____

9. Several people interviewed for the job. _____

10. Luckily, I watch the newspaper ads. _____

 Rewrite the sentences by changing the underlined verbs to the past tense.

11. Carmen's little dog will follow her everywhere.

_____

12. He will bark and jump at her heels.

_____

13. He walks along behind her, and he even travels in the car with her.

_____

Verb Tenses, p. 2

✳ **Complete each sentence by changing the verb to the tense shown in parentheses.**

14. arrive (future) Hillary _____ will arrive _____ tomorrow.

15. pick (future) Casey _____ her up at the airport.

16. walk (past) We _____ to the restaurant yesterday.

17. need (past) Jacy _____ to make reservations for dinner.

18. watch (present) Hillary _____ my children for me.

19. walk (future) We _____ to the center for a sightseeing tour.

20. seem (present) Leslie _____ very excited about Hillary's visit.

21. visit (past) Keisha _____ her cousin Tobi last week.

22. wash (past) Jason _____ his car before work today.

23. dance (present) Keisha _____ at that club every weekend.

24. train (future) I _____ for that job soon.

25. prepare (past) Suzanne _____ the entire meal.

26. start (past) Hiroshi _____ cooking for friends, too.

27. inform (future) Angela _____ her co-worker of the new rules.

✳ **Underline the verb or verb phrase in each sentence. Then write present, past, or future for the tense of each verb.**

28. My sister and her family <u>live</u> in a house near mine. _____ present _____

29. Sometimes I take my nieces to the library. _____

30. Often they play in front of my house. _____

31. One day Kara threw the ball very hard to Joslyn. _____

32. The ball sailed over Joslyn's head and into the street. _____

33. Joslyn ran toward the street. _____

34. I shouted to Joslyn. _____

35. Usually Joslyn listens to me. _____

36. I got the ball from the street. _____

37. My sister called for her to come home. _____

38. Next time they will play only in the backyard. _____

Principal Parts of Verbs

- The four principal parts of a verb are **present**, **present participle**, **past**, and **past participle**.
- Form the **present participle** of a regular verb by adding <u>ing</u> to the present. Use a form of the helping verb <u>be</u> (am, is, are).
- Form the present participle of a regular verb ending in <u>e</u> by dropping the final <u>e</u> before adding ing.
- Form the **past** and **past participle** of a regular verb by adding <u>d</u> or <u>ed</u> to the present. Use a form of the helping verb <u>have</u> (have, has, had) to form the past participle.
- Form the past and past participle of most regular verbs ending in <u>y</u> by changing the <u>y</u> to i before adding ed.

Present	Present Participle	Past	Past Participle
laugh	(is) laughing	laughed	(has) laughed
bake	(is) baking	baked	(has) baked
hurry	(is) hurrying	hurried	(has) hurried
hop	(is) hopping	hopped	(has) hopped

Write the present participle, past, and past participle for each verb.

PRESENT	PRESENT PARTICIPLE	PAST	PAST PARTICIPLE
1. stop	(is) stopping	stopped	(has) stopped
2. listen			
3. carry			
4. help			
5. start			
6. borrow			
7. call			
8. receive			
9. hope			
10. illustrate			
11. divide			
12. change			
13. live			
14. iron			
15. collect			

Name _____   Date _____

Irregular Verbs

- To form the past and past participle of some **irregular verbs,** change the vowels (or vowel sounds) of the present.
- To form the past participle of some irregular verbs, add a final <u>n</u> sound (n, en, ne).
- A dictionary shows the principal parts of irregular verbs.

EXAMPLES:

Present	Present Participle	Past	Past Participle
drink	(is) drinking	drank	(has) drunk (change vowels)
bite	(is) biting	bit	(has) bitten (change vowel sound and add final <u>n</u>)
do	(is) doing	did	(has) done (add final <u>ne</u>)

✵ **Write the principal parts of each verb. You may use a dictionary if necessary.**

PRESENT	PRESENT PARTICIPLE	PAST	PAST PARTICIPLE
1. come	(is) coming	came	(has) come
2. eat	_____	_____	_____
3. see	_____	_____	_____
4. take	_____	_____	_____

✵ **Complete each sentence with the correct form of the verb in parentheses.**

5. (see)   I never _____saw_____ a waterfall so steep before.

6. (take)   Lauren is _____ the hammer with her.

7. (see)   We are _____ the end of the passenger train.

8. (take)   Haven't you _____ your lunch break yet?

9. (eat)   Have you ever _____ a spiced olive?

10. (take)   On their last trip, Carey _____ all the photographs.

11. (do)   Who _____ the landscaping around this building last year?

12. (do)   We have _____ a lot of outside reading on the topic for discussion.

13. (come)   People have _____ from around the world to see Carlsbad Caverns.

14. (eat)   Last year on vacation we _____ unusual foods in every part of the country.

15. (see)   Thomas, you should have _____ the last game.

16. (come)   Most of the joggers _____ down this trail in the last race.

Language: Usage and Practice HS, SV 1419027867

Name _____ Date _____

Irregular Verbs, p. 2

 Write the principal parts of each verb. You may use a dictionary.

PRESENT	PRESENT PARTICIPLE	PAST	PAST PARTICIPLE
17. begin	_____	_____	_____
18. go	_____	_____	_____
19. drive	_____	_____	_____
20. give	_____	_____	_____
21. run	_____	_____	_____

 Complete each sentence with the correct form of the verb in parentheses.

22. (give)   My friend _____ this poem to me.

23. (run)   The excited children _____ down the street.

24. (go)   Work on the new building had _____ well until now.

25. (begin)   I _____ this project yesterday.

26. (drive)   Aren't you _____ a new car?

27. (drive)   Samuel, have you ever _____ a car?

28. (give)   Gwendolyn Brooks has _____ us many interesting poems.

29. (begin)   The supervisor of the crew is _____ to explain the work orders.

30. (run)   Rachel, have you _____ into Sarah?

31. (go)   The little girl _____ to visit her grandparents last week.

32. (begin)   That problem _____ last year.

33. (give)   My friends have _____ me a present for my birthday.

34. (go)   The weatherman says it is _____ to rain.

35. (run)   After the rumble of thunder, Jarred _____ to get out of the rain.

36. (give)   Mrs. Williams has _____ me a job on Saturday afternoons.

37. (give)   Donell, who _____ you this watch?

38. (begin)   We haven't _____ work on the new roof yet.

39. (drive)   We _____ to work in the van this morning.

40. (begin)   Scott _____ to rake the leaves early this fall.

41. (run)   Michelle is _____ for election to the school board.

Language: Usage and Practice HS, SV 1419027867

Name _____   Date _____

More Irregular Verbs

❋ **Write the principal parts of each verb. You may use a dictionary.**

PRESENT	PRESENT PARTICIPLE	PAST	PAST PARTICIPLE
1. grow	_____	_____	_____
2. know	_____	_____	_____
3. ring	_____	_____	_____
4. sing	_____	_____	_____
5. speak	_____	_____	_____

❋ **Complete each sentence with the correct form of the verb in parentheses.**

6. (sing)   Have you ever _____ a solo?

7. (grow)   Last night at dusk, my eyes _____ accustomed to the dark.

8. (know)   On last week's test, Rob _____ the answer before anyone.

9. (grow)   It has _____ very cold during the last hour.

10. (sing)   Ricardo is _____, although his throat is sore.

11. (ring)   Why hasn't the bell _____?

12. (grow)   Lettuce has _____ in China for many years.

13. (speak)   Cyndi _____ to her boss yesterday.

14. (ring)   The mail carrier _____ the doorbell at the vacant house several times.

15. (speak)   Has Rafael _____ to you about his promotion?

16. (speak)   A traffic officer is _____ to a group of concerned citizens.

17. (sing)   Natasha and her sister _____ on a local TV program last week.

18. (know)   We have _____ the members of that family a long time.

19. (ring)   The mission bells _____ each morning last week.

20. (speak)   Have you _____ to your teacher yet?

21. (grow)   Chet, I believe you have _____ a prize-winning rose.

22. (know)   We have _____ Roberto's brother for three years.

23. (grow)   Because of the rain, the grass is _____ rapidly.

24. (ring)   The phone _____ frequently during my favorite television show last night.

25. (speak)   My mother has _____ of you quite often, Mrs. Brown.

Unit 3: Grammar and Usage
Language: Usage and Practice HS, SV 1419027867

More Irregular Verbs, p. 2

 Write the principal parts of each verb. You may use a dictionary.

PRESENT	PRESENT PARTICIPLE	PAST	PAST PARTICIPLE
26. blow	_____	_____	_____
27. break	_____	_____	_____
28. choose	_____	_____	_____
29. draw	_____	_____	_____
30. fly	_____	_____	_____

Complete each sentence with the correct form of the verb in parentheses.

31. (draw)   Kim has _____ many cartoons for the daily paper.

32. (blow)   Yesterday's storm _____ tumbleweeds across the prairie.

33. (fly)   The tiny mockingbird is _____ from its nest.

34. (choose)   John _____ only fresh vegetables for last night's salad.

35. (choose)   Our bowling club has _____ new officers.

36. (blow)   Has the five o'clock whistle _____?

37. (break)   I accidentally _____ my sister's antique vase.

38. (break)   Her promise had not been _____.

39. (choose)   The coach is _____ the lineup for today's game.

40. (draw)   A famous artist _____ these old sketches.

41. (break)   One of the windows in the factory had _____ during the storm.

42. (break)   The handle of my hammer _____ while I was using it.

43. (choose)   Has anyone _____ the menu for our lunch?

44. (fly)   Shannon had _____ to Rochester, New York.

45. (break)   Those pipes _____ last February.

46. (choose)   Do you think I have _____ wisely?

47. (break)   They _____ our winning streak last week.

48. (draw)   Have you _____ a map to your house, Leo?

49. (break)   Who is _____ these windows?

50. (draw)   The architect has _____ the plans for the new house.

Name ______________________________ Date ______________________________

Tense Progression

- When verbs are used in more than one part of a sentence, they must work together to show the correct time order. This is called **tense progression.**
- The tense of the second verb must make sense with the tense of the first verb.

EXAMPLES:

Before I **had eaten**, I **was** hungry.	(correct)
Before I **had eaten**, I **am** hungry.	(incorrect)
When I **ate** lunch, I **felt** full.	(correct)
When I **ate** lunch, I **feel** full.	(incorrect)
If I **have been eating**, I **don't** swim.	(correct)
If I **have been eating**, I **didn't** swim.	(incorrect)
After I **have rested**, I **will swim**.	(correct)
After I **have rested**, I **swam**.	(incorrect)

Complete each sentence with the correct tense of the verb in parentheses. The sentences should tell a story.

1. (take) Ms. Reyna ____________ her car in for repairs after it began overheating.
2. (has) She asked the mechanic if he ____________ time to look at the car that day.
3. (is) He said he ____________ busy until the next week.
4. (take) If she has time, she ____________ it in to the shop next Wednesday.
5. (pick) She ____________ up the car after he has worked on it.
6. (buy) Ms. Reyna has had trouble with the car since she ____________ it.
7. (hope) She ____________ it will not overheat after it is repaired.

Rewrite each sentence by correcting the tense progression.

8. When Reggie shopped for groceries, he buys fresh fruits and vegetables.

____

9. The broccoli looked very fresh, but the squash doesn't.

____

10. After he got home with the food, he starts to make dinner.

____

11. Then Carla comes home, and they sat down to eat.

____

12. They clean up the kitchen together after they had finished eating.

____

13. Then Reggie turned on the television and watches a movie.

____

14. Carla fell asleep as soon as she sits down.

____

Using *Is* or *Are* and *Was* or *Were*

- Use <u>is</u> and <u>was</u> with one person, place, or thing.
- Use <u>are</u> and <u>were</u> with more than one person, place, or thing.
    EXAMPLES:
        Roberto **is** a cook now.
        He **was** a waiter for a while.
        His <u>brothers</u> **are** bakers.
        <u>They</u> **were** all waiters once.
- Find the subject and then choose the verb that agrees with it.
    EXAMPLES:
        The <u>lamp</u> with the broken bulbs **is** in Etta's office.
        The <u>tools</u> that Mike uses **are** in his toolbox.
- Always use <u>are</u> and <u>were</u> with the pronoun <u>you</u>.
    EXAMPLES:
        <u>You</u> **are** my best friend.
        <u>You</u> **were** late today.

 Underline the verb in parentheses that agrees with the subject of each sentence.

1. The box you ordered (is, are) finally here.
2. Jennifer (is, are) the name of three women in our department.
3. The chance of rain showers tomorrow (is, are) 50 percent.
4. Senator Thompson (is, are) going to speak today.
5. The games you asked me to bring (is, are) in the car.
6. An easier way to make parts (is, are) possible.
7. Two of these chairs (is, are) damaged.
8. (Is, Are) these brick houses for sale, too?
9. Kelly, (is, are) this your car?
10. A mob of busy shoppers (is, are) at the going-out-of-business sale.
11. Juan and I (was, were) afraid that Carlos (was, were) late again.
12. (Was, Were) you talking to Justin this afternoon?
13. A group of truck drivers (was, were) in the cafe.
14. Many trees that had to be cut down (was, were) diseased.
15. Several visitors (was, were) here this afternoon.
16. Hanna, (wasn't, weren't) you interested in working overtime?
17. Why (wasn't, weren't) these dishes washed last night?
18. The mistakes in punctuation (was, were) too numerous to fix.
19. Barry and Sara (wasn't, weren't) able to help.
20. A large tray of sandwiches (was, were) on the table.
21. Each slide (was, were) ready for the presentation.
22. One of my sisters (was, were) in a nursing program.
23. Each of the daily reports (was, were) in the office before noon.
24. (Was, Were) you planning to go to the supermarket today?
25. The swans and ducks in the pond (was, were) noisy.
26. (Wasn't, Weren't) you at the annual meeting, Bart?

Using *There Is* or *There Are* and *There Was* or *There Were*

> - Use <u>there is</u> or <u>there was</u> with one person, place, or thing.
> - Use <u>there are</u> or <u>there were</u> with more than one person, place, or thing.
>   EXAMPLES:
>   **There is** a job opening today.
>   **There are** several vacancies.
>   **There was** an opening last week.
>   **There were** several openings last week.

 Underline the correct words to complete each sentence.

1. (There is, <u>There are</u>) twelve women and eight men in our office.
2. (There was, There were) no one at home when we called.
3. (There was, There were) many new police officers hired last month.
4. (There was, There were) two broken jars in the case.
5. (There is, There are) too many boxes in this warehouse.
6. (There was, There were) only ten passengers on the bus.
7. (There was, There were) too many people late this morning.
8. (There was, There were) sixteen people waiting in line.
9. I'm sure (there is, there are) no letters for me.
10. (There is, There are) no letters in the mailbox.
11. (There is, There are) tools scattered around on every shelf.
12. (There is, There are) no crackers in the box.
13. (There is, There are) not enough money to repaint the building and put on a new roof.
14. (There is, There are) many trained workers available now.
15. (There is, There are) three new chairs to be delivered today.
16. (There is, There are) only one showcase in the hall.
17. (There is, There are) many brick houses in our town.
18. (There is, There are) many ways to get the job done.
19. (There was, There were) ten guests at our party.
20. (There is, There are) three checks to be deposited.
21. (There is, There are) no milk left in this carton.
22. (There was, There were) several buses at the bus stop.
23. (There was, There were) very little rain this year.
24. (There was, There were) several hundred people delayed by the traffic.
25. (There was, There were) two messages left for you.
26. (There was, There were) few people in line at the bank.
27. (There is, There are) many interesting things to see in Denver, Colorado.
28. I thought (there was, there were) a dozen or more eggs in the refrigerator.
29. (There is, There are) many people interested in running for office.

Name _____   Date _____

Using Forms of *Do*

- <u>Don't</u> is the contraction of <u>do</u> and <u>not</u>.
- Use <u>don't</u> with plural nouns and with the pronouns <u>I</u>, <u>you</u>, <u>we</u>, and <u>they</u>.
- <u>Don't</u> is used as a helping verb.
    EXAMPLES:
        Our relatives **don't** <u>visit</u> very often.
        We **don't** <u>get</u> by to see them much, either.
- <u>Doesn't</u> is the contraction of <u>does</u> and <u>not</u>.
- Use <u>doesn't</u> with singular nouns and the pronouns <u>he</u>, <u>she</u>, and <u>it</u>.
- <u>Doesn't</u> is also used as a helping verb.
    EXAMPLES:
        He **doesn't** <u>want</u> to go.
        But Rachel **does**.
- Did and <u>done</u> are past tense verbs. With <u>done</u>, use a form of <u>has</u> (have, has, or had).
    EXAMPLES:
        Hallie **did** a great job.
        Angie <u>has</u> **done** a great job, too.

 Underline the correct verb in parentheses to complete each sentence.

1. Why (doesn't, don't) Lonna have the car keys?

2. Show me the way you (did, done) it.

3. Have the three of you (did, done) most of the work?

4. Why (doesn't, don't) she cash a check today?

5. Please show me what damage the storm (did, done).

6. (Doesn't, Don't) the workers on the morning shift do a fine job?

7. Have the new owners of our building (did, done) anything about the plumbing?

8. (Doesn't, Don't) those apples look delicious?

9. Christine (doesn't, don't) want to do the spring cleaning this week.

10. The washer and the dryer (doesn't, don't) work.

11. Audrey, have you (did, done) your homework today?

12. Who (did, done) this fine job of painting?

13. (Doesn't, Don't) the tile in the new kitchen look nice?

14. (Doesn't, Don't) their daughter go to preschool?

15. He has (did, done) me a great favor.

16. I will help even if he (doesn't, don't).

17. I (doesn't, don't) want you to go if you'd rather stay here.

18. Why (doesn't, don't) he apply for the job?

19. Jonathan's parents (doesn't, don't) want him to miss school.

20. Eleanor, how (did, done) you get so much done in such a short time?

21. We (doesn't, don't) know when the furniture will be delivered.

22. Mr. and Mrs. Wang have (did, done) all of the work themselves.

23. Marina, (doesn't, don't) she already have her GED?

24. (Doesn't, Don't) forget to do the laundry, April.

Language: Usage and Practice HS, SV 1419027867

Name _____ Date _____

Using *Lie* or *Lay*

- Lie means "to recline" or "to occupy a certain place."
- Lay means "to place."
- Here are the principal parts of both verbs.

Present	Present Participle	Past	Past Participle
lie	(is) lying	lay	(has) lain
lay	(is) laying	laid	(has) laid

EXAMPLES:
The baby **lies** in her crib.
Her diapers **lie** on the chest.
Lay a diaper out first.
Then **lay** the baby down.

 Underline the correct word in parentheses to complete each sentence.

1. Canada (lays, lies) to the north of the United States.

2. (Lay, Lie) these books on the table.

3. My dog is (laying, lying) on the floor.

4. The nurse asked Stan to (lay, lie) down on the examining table.

5. Herman had (lain, laid) the morning paper by his plate.

6. She has (lain, laid) the letter on the edge of her desk.

7. After that long trip, I had to (lie, lay) down for a while.

8. Because of the accident, he can't (lay, lie) on his left side.

9. Li-ming (lay, laid) her book aside and went to the door.

10. Where does the Indian Ocean (lay, lie)?

11. The campers had (laid, lain) in their sleeping bags all night long.

12. I (lay, laid) in bed with the flu for almost a week.

13. California (lays, lies) to the east of the Pacific Ocean.

14. Why have you (laid, lain) in the sun all day?

15. He (laid, lay) awake every night.

16. Please (lie, lay) the dishes aside for now.

17. Marta (lay, laid) the magazines on the table when she finished reading them.

18. After eating that heavy meal, the whole family is (laying, lying) down for a nap.

19. I found the reports (laying, lying) on her desk under some other papers.

20. He has been (laying, lying) there for two hours.

21. The dog had (lain, laid) its left paw on the man's knee.

22. Jenna has (laid, lain) her pictures on the bed.

23. Europe (lays, lies) to the north of Africa.

24. (Lie, Lay) the toy in the crib.

25. He is (laying, lying) on the sofa because he hurt his back.

26. Rochelle likes to (lie, lay) all the utensils out on the counter before she cooks.

27. Evan is (laying, lying) a trap in his attic.

Using *Sit* or *Set*

- Sit means "to take a resting position."
- Set means "to place."
- Here are the principal parts of both verbs.

Present	Present Participle	Past	Past Participle
sit	(is) sitting	sat	(has) sat
set	(is) setting	set	(has) set

EXAMPLES:
Let's **sit** on this row.
He **sat** beside me at the movie.
First **set** the table.
Then **set** out the flowers.

 Underline the correct verb in parentheses to complete each sentence.

1. Please (sit, set) down, Ms. Blakeney.

2. Where should we (sit, set) the television?

3. Where do you (sit, set)?

4. Pam, please (sit, set) those plants out this afternoon.

5. (Sit, Set) the groceries on the counter.

6. Mr. Romero usually (sits, sets) on this side of the table.

7. Please come and (sit, set) your books down on that desk.

8. Trent (sat, set) by the window.

9. Does he (sit, set) in this seat?

10. Why don't you (sit, set) over here?

11. Please (sit, set) this table in the conference room.

12. Where do you prefer to (sit, set)?

13. The little girl is (sitting, setting) in the high chair.

14. In a theater I always like to (sit, set) near the aisle.

15. I (sat, set) in a reserved seat at the last game.

16. Alberto, please (sit, set) next to me.

17. With tired sighs, we (sat, set) down on the couch.

18. Jacob, have you (sit, set) out the blueprints?

19. The workers (sat, set) stone upon stone.

20. I like to (sit, set) in a window seat on a plane so I can see.

21. Please (sit, set) these chairs on the rug.

22. Troy has (sat, set) his work aside.

23. All the passengers are (sitting, setting) quietly while the flat tire is fixed.

24. Mark (sat, set) the dirty clothes on top of the washing machine.

25. Why did you (set, sit) in the corner?

26. Rhonda asked Ray where he wanted to (set, sit).

27. Let's ask Amelia why she (sets, sits) her books on the floor.

28. The audience (set, sat) in the theater while the stagehands (sat, set) the stage for the play.

Name _____ Date _____

Using *Learn* or *Teach*

- Learn means "to acquire knowledge."
- Teach means "to give knowledge to" or "to instruct."
- Here are the principal parts of both verbs.

Present	Present Participle	Past	Past Participle
learn	(is) learning	learned	(has) learned
teach	(is) teaching	taught	(has) taught

EXAMPLES:
I want to **learn** how to tap dance.
Please **teach** me what you know about it.

 Complete each sentence with <u>teach</u> or <u>learn</u>.

1. I think he will _____ me quickly.

2. I would like to _____ to change the spark plugs on my car.

3. Did the salesperson _____ you how to install your new oven?

4. The employees are going to _____ about their new benefits.

5. Will you _____ me to drive a stick shift?

6. My brother is going to _____ his son to skate.

7. Would you like to _____ the safety rules to them?

8. No one can _____ you if you don't try to _____.

9. I'd like to _____ children someday.

 Underline the correct word in parentheses to complete each sentence.

10. The paramedic is (learning, teaching) us CPR.

11. You should (learn, teach) to do CPR, too.

12. The driving instructor (learned, taught) us the importance of wearing seat belts.

13. Let me (learn, teach) you a shorter way to do this.

14. If you (learn, teach) me how to operate this machine, I'll try to (learn, teach) quickly.

15. Teri, did you (learn, teach) to type in school, or did you (learn, teach) yourself?

16. Marcy has (learned, taught) several people to cook Chinese food.

17. You can (learn, teach) some animals to do tricks more easily than others.

18. The first-aid course has (learned, taught) me important procedures.

19. Who (learned, taught) you how to drive a car?

20. Claire is (learning, teaching) how to program her computer this August.

21. Please (learn, teach) me the correct way to fill out this application.

22. He is (learning, teaching) his son to tie his shoes.

23. I have (taught, learned) how to do my taxes from Mr. Burner.

Name _____ Date _____

Subject Pronouns

> - A **pronoun** is a word used in place of a noun.
> - A **subject pronoun** is the subject or part of the subject of a sentence.
> - The subject pronouns are I, you, he, she, it, we, and they.
>   EXAMPLE: **It** has beautiful wings.
> - With other pronouns or nouns, the pronoun I comes last.
>   EXAMPLE: Marie and **I** caught a butterfly.

 Underline the correct pronouns in parentheses to complete the sentences.

1. Mason and (I, me) helped repair the car.

2. (She, Her) and I are going to the movies.

3. Why can't Leigh and (I, me) go with them?

4. (She, Her) and Chip skated all afternoon.

5. Jadyn and (I, me) are going to Chicago tomorrow.

6. (He, Him) played volleyball this morning.

7. Lindsey and (he, him) were five minutes late yesterday morning.

8. (She, Her) and (I, me) spent an hour in the public library.

9. Mario and (I, me) worked until nine o'clock.

10. (He, Him) and Yuri are going over there now.

11. May (we, us) carry your packages?

12. (They, Them) are buying some groceries for the picnic.

13. Kara and (I, me) are going with her to the park.

14. (It, Them) slowed down and came to a stop at the corner.

15. (She and I, I and she) drive to work together in a carpool.

16. (He, Him) is the owner of the suitcase.

17. Crystal and (I, me) are on the same shift.

18. (I and he, He and I) started a neighborhood watch on our street.

19. (We, Us) are planning a garage sale.

20. (They, Them) are going to see a play.

21. Is (she, her) your favorite singer?

22. Either Marty or (I, me) would be happy to help you.

23. (We, Us) work at the post office.

24. (She, Her) and Sulema are painting the front porch.

 Write a sentence about you and another person. Use subject pronouns.

25. _____

Object Pronouns

- The **object pronouns** are <u>me</u>, <u>you</u>, <u>him</u>, <u>her</u>, <u>it</u>, <u>us</u>, and <u>them</u>.
- An object pronoun comes after an action verb or after a preposition (such as <u>after</u>, <u>by</u>, <u>for</u>, <u>from</u>, <u>in</u>, <u>to</u>, or <u>with</u>).
  EXAMPLES:
  The mailman gave **me** the letters.
  I gave **them** to my boss.
  The package was for **her**.
  She shared **it** with **us**.
- The object pronoun <u>me</u> comes last with other pronouns or nouns.
  EXAMPLE: The magazines were for Kay and **me**.

 Underline the correct pronouns in parentheses to complete the sentences.

1. Vince, are you going with Elayne and (I, me)?

2. Scott invited Pat and (I, me) to one of the club picnics.

3. I am going to talk to Mandy and (she, her) about the problem.

4. Mrs. Wong told (us, we) to collect her old magazines.

5. I went with Mrs. Kriger and (she, her) to the hobby show.

6. That dinner was prepared by (them, they).

7. Andrew asked (Vince and me, me and Vince) to go to the baseball game.

8. Amelia and Jordan congratulated (he, him).

9. Miss Carr praised (him, he) for his work.

10. Will you talk to (she, her) about the trip?

11. Ben, can you go with Renee and (I, me)?

12. The mechanic asked (us, we) about buying a new muffler for the car.

13. Give the package to (Tracy and me, me and Tracy).

14. They brought the problem to (we, us).

15. The problem was too hard for (they, them) to solve.

16. Rick gave (I, me) his old computer equipment.

17. Ms. Planter is showing (we, us) how to plant a vegetable garden.

18. Please inform (he, him) of the change of plans.

19. Bert offered to help Shonna and (I, me) hang the curtains.

20. That car belongs to (he, him).

21. Karl didn't see (they, them).

22. Deena asked him to take a picture of (we, us).

23. Please wait for (she, her) after work.

24. She likes to go grocery shopping with (he, him).

25. Hand the packages to (they, them).

26. Was this really built by (she, her)?

27. Would you like to play basketball with (we, us)?

Name _____   Date _____

Possessive Pronouns

- A **possessive pronoun** shows ownership.
- The possessive pronouns <u>mine</u>, <u>yours</u>, <u>hers</u>, <u>ours</u>, and <u>theirs</u> stand alone.
  EXAMPLES:
  That coat is **mine**.
  Yours is on the chair.
- The possessive pronouns <u>my</u>, <u>your</u>, <u>her</u>, <u>its</u>, <u>our</u>, and <u>their</u> come before nouns.
  EXAMPLES:
  Her new **car** is red.
  Our black **car** is the same model.
- The possessive pronoun <u>his</u> may stand alone or come before a noun.
  EXAMPLES:
  That is **his** dog.
  The dog is **his**.

 Underline the possessive pronouns in each sentence.

1. Lora bought <u>her</u> bracelet at the mall. Carri bought <u>hers</u> there, too.

2. Dave met his wife playing soccer. I met mine at work.

3. New applicants should bring their work history. Is this yours?

4. The referee blew her whistle.

5. The children took their books on the trip. Kelly and Ann read theirs in the car.

6. Musician Louis Armstrong was famous for his smile.

7. He entered his radio-controlled airplane in the contest.

8. Dan wanted to borrow our book, but many of its pages were missing.

9. My aunt and uncle have sold their repair shop.

10. Carpenter ants build their nests in wood.

11. How did the state of Florida get its name?

12. My family collects stamps. Ahmad likes our Russian collection best.

13. The robin built its nest in our oak tree.

14. An evergreen tree keeps its leaves in the winter.

15. Cristen sprained her ankle while climbing a ladder.

16. She drove her car to the new warehouse.

17. Where is your umbrella? Sabrina borrowed mine.

18. Isn't Alaska noted for its salmon?

19. Travis brought his mother a beautiful shawl from India.

20. Gina, where is your calendar? Jim can't find ours.

 Write two sentences using the possessive pronouns <u>my</u> and <u>mine</u> or <u>our</u> and <u>ours</u>.

21. _____

22. _____

Unit 3: Grammar and Usage
Language: Usage and Practice HS, SV 1419027867

Name _____ Date _____

Indefinite Pronouns

- An **indefinite pronoun** does not refer to a specific person or thing.
  EXAMPLE: **Someone** is talking about travel plans.
- These indefinite pronouns are singular. They take singular verbs.
anybody	anyone	anything	each	everyone
everybody	everything	nobody	no one	nothing
somebody	someone	something		
  EXAMPLE: **Everybody is** looking forward to the trip.
- These indefinite pronouns are plural. They take plural verbs.
both	few	many	several	some
  EXAMPLES:
  Several of us **have** already paid.
  Many are going for the second time.
- These indefinite pronouns are negative.
nobody	no one	nothing
  EXAMPLE: **Nobody** has a ticket.

 Underline the indefinite pronoun in each sentence.

1. <u>Everyone</u> helped complete the project.

2. Is somebody waiting for you?

3. Anything is possible.

4. Something arrived in the mail.

5. Everybody looked tired.

6. No one was willing to work longer.

7. Does anyone have a quarter?

8. Both of us were tired.

9. Nothing was dry yet.

10. Does anybody want to go swimming?

11. Someone should speak up.

12. Everybody is hungry now.

13. Each of the cars was black.

14. Some of the patients rest in the afternoon.

15. Several were empty.

16. No one remembered to bring it.

17. Everyone started to feel nervous.

18. Nobody admitted to being afraid.

19. Everything will be explained.

20. Is anything missing?

 Complete each sentence with an indefinite pronoun.

21. _____ Something _____ from my desk has disappeared.

22. Is _____ going to teach you how to run the computer?

23. Every person in our district voted on Election Day. _____ voted early.

24. She tried to call, but _____ answered the phone.

25. Does _____ remember the address?

26. There is _____ here to see you.

27. Would _____ like a piece of cake?

28. _____ of the clocks are slow.

Language: Usage and Practice HS, SV 1419027867

Name _____   Date _____

Antecedents

- An **antecedent** is the word to which a pronoun refers.
- A pronoun must agree with its antecedent in gender (masculine or feminine).
    EXAMPLES:
        Blanca took **her** broken watch to the jewelry store.
        Joe drove **his** truck to the auto supply store.
- A pronoun must agree with its antecedent in number (singular or plural).
    EXAMPLES:
        Each of the gardens has **its** own fountain.
        Dogs are dangerous if **they** bite.
- When two or more antecedents are joined by <u>or</u> or <u>nor</u>, the pronoun is singular.
    EXAMPLES:
        Javier **or** Juan threw down **his** jacket.
        Neither Lila **nor** Elena wanted **her** lunch.
- When two or more antecedents are joined by **and**, the pronoun is plural.
    EXAMPLE: Mr. **and** Mrs. Delgado made up **their** own minds.

 Underline each pronoun and circle the antecedents.

1. (Jenna) and (Rob) planned a surprise party for <u>their</u> friend Sara.

2. Jenna invited her friends, and Rob invited his friends.

3. The friends said that they would come.

4. When Rob wrapped the last present, he and Jenna ate dinner.

5. After dinner, Jenna and Rob returned to their party planning.

6. Jenna asked Rob to help her with the decorations.

7. Jenna put colored streamers on her walls.

8. Rob baked a chocolate cake and put icing on it.

9. When Sara arrived, she was completely surprised.

10. Rob and Jenna knew all their hard work had paid off.

 Underline the correct word in parentheses to complete each sentence.

11. Domingo left (their, <u>his</u>) book on the counter.

12. Both of the passengers forgot to put on (her, their) seat belts.

13. The squirrel found (its, their) own comfortable spot on the oak limb.

14. Two of the sisters think that (they, she) need a vacation.

15. Elena or Mandy will take (their, her) turn next.

16. The Lichters and (their, his) neighbors often play cards together.

17. Each of the mechanics brought (her, their) own tools.

18. Rachel and Sameera are the first ones to turn in (their, her) time cards.

19. Neither Frank nor Marco did the chores (he, they) promised to do.

20. Two groups are writing (its, their) own project proposals.

Unit 3: Grammar and Usage
Language: Usage and Practice HS, SV 1419027867

Name _____ Date _____

Pronouns with *Self* and *Selves*

- Pronouns ending in <u>self</u> are singular. Pronouns ending in <u>selves</u> are plural. <u>Hisself</u> and <u>theirselves</u> are not words.
    - **Singular:** myself, herself, himself, itself, yourself, oneself
    - **Plural:** yourselves, themselves, ourselves
- A <u>self</u> pronoun is used to tell about or emphasize another pronoun or noun.
- It comes after an action verb or a preposition when it tells about (reflects back to) a noun or pronoun.
- It comes after a noun or pronoun for emphasis.
    - EXAMPLES:
        - <u>Georgia</u> <u>bought</u> **herself** a new coat.
        - **We** went shopping by **ourselves**.
        - **Ian himself** fixed the leak.
- A <u>self</u> pronoun should not be used when an object pronoun is needed.
    - EXAMPLES:
        - They asked Tom and **me** to the party.   (correct)
        - They asked Tom and myself to the party.   (incorrect)
- A <u>self</u> pronoun should not be used as a subject.
    - EXAMPLES:
        - Tanya and **I** like hiking.   (correct)
        - Tanya and **myself** like hiking.   (incorrect)

 Underline the correct pronoun in parentheses to complete each sentence.

1. The children took care of (<u>themselves</u>, himself) until their parents arrived.

2. I'm glad to see that Nekesia is pleased with (herself, she).

3. Rico and (myself, I) will make all the arrangements for the meeting.

4. I always try to be honest with (me, myself).

5. Cal hit (he, himself) with a hammer.

6. Neither Nick nor Oscar blamed (himself, themselves).

7. (Ourselves, We) are working together to make everyone feel safe.

8. One should think of others as well as (oneself, themselves).

9. Will the guests help (themselves, himself) to the refreshments?

10. The movie (itself, herself) was not very good, but the acting was great.

11. Young girls often want to cook dinner by (herself, themselves).

12. Jason and (I, myself) are both looking for night jobs.

13. The boss (herself, she) delivered the paychecks.

14. Andy wanted to bake the cake (he, himself), but he ran out of time.

15. We had a hard time running the new computer by (ourselves, himself).

16. Shannon sent birthday cards to both Lawonda and (myself, me).

17. (I myself, Myself) have decided to move to a furnished apartment.

18. Will you help (myself, me) with this project?

Name _____   Date _____

Relative Pronouns *Who, Which,* and *That*

- A **relative pronoun** connects an antecedent with another part of a sentence.
- The relative pronouns are who, which, and that. Who and forms of who refer only to people. Which refers only to things. That refers either to people or things.
    EXAMPLES:
        It was **Elsa who** did it.
        The **cake, which** Jeffrey made for Martha, was delicious.
        A sedan is the kind of **car that** I like.
        The winner will be the **one that** finishes first.
- In formal writing, who and whoever are used as subjects. Whom and whomever are used as objects. Whose is used as a possessive.
    EXAMPLES:
        Is he the one **who** called in sick this morning?
        I hope that **whoever** sees the ring returns it.
        The salesman to **whom** you talked is not here today.
        Are you the one **whose** ring is missing?

 Underline the correct relative pronoun in each sentence.

1. The bowler's ball, (that, which) was custom made, fell in the gutter.

2. Hector is the man (who, which) telephoned us yesterday.

3. This is the kind of car (who, that) I like to drive.

4. She is a person (that, which) can be counted on to help.

5. Is Ming the one (that, which) was elected to organize the campaign?

6. Crissi, (who, which) lost her little dog Rex, is very upset.

7. Ms. Cruz is a storyteller (which, who) delights in amusing her audience.

 Underline the correct formal form of who for each sentence.

8. (who, whom) Rasheed was the man _____ painted that beautiful mural.

9. (who, whom) For _____ did you buy that gift?

10. (Whoever, Whomever) _____ ordered this equipment should sign for it.

11. (who, whose) Chan is the one _____ is coming to the reunion.

12. (who, whom) Mrs. Brodsky, with _____ I bowled last week, won the trophy.

13. (who, whom) I asked Sybil, _____ is my best friend, about my new hairstyle.

14. (who, whose) That is the kind of friend _____ opinion I value.

15. (who, whom) To _____ do we give our tickets?

 Write two sentences that tell about people or places you know. Use who, which, and that.

_____

_____

Language: Usage and Practice HS, SV 1419027867

Using *Who* or *Whom*

- In formal English <u>who</u> is used as a subject, and <u>whom</u> is used as an object.
  EXAMPLES:
  Who is that singer?
  Is he the one **who** won a Grammy?
  To **whom** was it given?
  Whom was the song written by?

 Complete each sentence with <u>who</u> or <u>whom</u>.

1. _____ told you about our plans?

2. _____ is one of the greatest space scientists?

3. _____ did Mrs. Renzell send for?

4. _____ are those women in the hallway?

5. _____ is your dentist?

6. _____ is older, your son or your daughter?

7. To _____ is that package addressed?

8. For _____ shall I ask?

9. _____ do you think can take my place?

10. _____ is going to the party?

11. _____ have the people elected?

12. _____ does your daughter look like?

13. _____ is the best accountant in the office?

14. _____ is the new employee?

15. _____ should I get to tow the car?

16. The mechanic _____ I called can help you.

17. _____ are you waiting to see?

18. _____ should we select to represent us at the meeting?

19. _____ told you about Lyman's operation?

20. _____ did he call?

21. Do you know _____ sat next to me?

22. _____ wants to buy a breakfast taco?

23. The woman _____ sells them is in Mr. Gregg's office.

Name _____ Date _____

Adjectives

- An **adjective** is a word that describes a noun or a pronoun.
    EXAMPLES:
        Loud music was playing.
        She was **late**.
- Adjectives usually tell what kind, which one, how many, or how much.
    EXAMPLES: **white** roses   **every** hammer   **fifteen** stamps   **some** money
- The words a, an, and the are also adjectives. They are called **articles**.
- Use a before a word beginning with a consonant sound.
- Use an before a word beginning with a vowel sound.
    EXAMPLES:
        An apple tree is **a** thing of beauty.
        The stupid apple tree blocked my view.

 Choose an adjective from the box to describe each noun.

| brave | foolish | many | shiny | enough |
| heavy | cold | more | fragrant | useful |

1. _____ firefighter   4. _____ students

2. _____ flower   5. _____ cars

3. _____ water   6. _____ answer

 Underline the adjectives in each sentence.

7. The spicy smell of warm soup filled the small kitchen.

8. A gusty wind blew the wet clothes from the clothesline.

9. She wanted to wear a long, blue dress with the new shoes.

10. I like to sleep under clean sheets and a soft, warm blanket.

11. She was tired after a long trip to the huge supermarket.

 Write a or an for each noun.

12. _____ train   16. _____ holiday   20. _____ umbrella

13. _____ iceberg   17. _____ astronaut   21. _____ mechanic

14. _____ orange   18. _____ welder

15. _____ error   19. _____ newspaper

 Write three adjectives to describe each noun.

22. summer _____ _____ _____

23. mountains _____ _____ _____

Language: Usage and Practice HS, SV 1419027867

Proper Adjectives

> • A **proper adjective** is formed from a proper noun. It always begins with a capital letter.
>   EXAMPLES:
>
> | Proper Noun | Proper Adjective |
> |-------------|------------------|
> | Poland | Polish |
> | Germany | German |
> | Paris | Parisian |

 Form a proper adjective from each proper noun. You may want to use a dictionary to check the spelling.

1. South America _____
2. Africa _____
3. England _____
4. Mexico _____
5. France _____
6. Russia _____
7. Puerto Rico _____
8. Rome _____
9. Alaska _____

10. Canada _____
11. Norway _____
12. Scotland _____
13. Ireland _____
14. China _____
15. Spain _____
16. Italy _____
17. Hawaii _____
18. Japan _____

 Write sentences using ten proper adjectives from the exercise above.

19. _____
20. _____
21. _____
22. _____
23. _____
24. _____
25. _____
26. _____
27. _____
28. _____

Language: Usage and Practice HS, SV 1419027867

Name _____ Date _____

Demonstrative Adjectives

- A **demonstrative adjective** points out a specific person or thing.
- This and that describe singular nouns. This refers to a nearby person or thing; that refers to a person or thing farther away.
  - EXAMPLES:
    - **This** pasta is delicious.
    - **That** road leads out of town.
- These and those describe plural nouns. These refers to nearby people or things; those refers to people or things farther away.
  - EXAMPLES:
    - **These** sunglasses are dark.
    - **Those** plants are growing well.
- Them is a pronoun. It cannot be used as an adjective.
  - EXAMPLES:
    - I like **them**.   (correct)
    - I like **them** apples.   (incorrect)

 Underline the correct word in parentheses to complete each sentence.

1. Please hand me one of (those, them) pencils.

2. Who are (those, them) new employees?

3. Was the article about (these, them) engines?

4. Have you heard (those, them) harmonica players?

5. (These, Them) ten problems are very difficult.

6. I do not like (that, those) loud music.

7. I need (this, these) kind of pencil to do my work.

8. (Those, Them) boots are too small for you.

9. Where did you buy (those, them) cantaloupes?

10. Most people like (that, those) kind of mystery story.

11. Please look carefully for (those, them) receipts.

12. Ashley, please copy (these, them) reports.

13. (Those, Them) machines are very difficult to operate.

14. (Those, Them) buildings are not open to the public.

15. Where did you find (that, those) uniform?

16. Please seat (these, them) guests.

17. Jeromy lives in (this, these) part of town.

18. (Those, Them) actors were convincing in their roles.

19. Kelly, I sent you (that, these) report when you asked for it.

20. Did you see (this, those) new mailboxes on the corner?

21. Marcos and Melissa painted (this, these) conference room.

22. (Those, Them) computer programs have been quite helpful.

23. Mr. Halsey, would you like to read (these, them) memos?

24. (This, These) sandals feel comfortable.

25. Is (that, those) phone number the correct one?

Comparing with Regular Adjectives

- An adjective has three forms: **positive**, **comparative**, and **superlative**.
- For regular adjectives (one-syllable and some two-syllable adjectives), add er to form the comparative and est to form the superlative.
    - EXAMPLE: rich   richer   richest

Here are some spelling rules for comparing most regular adjectives:
- If the adjective ends in e, drop the e and add er or est.
- If the adjective ends in y preceded by a consonant, change the y to i and add er or est.
- If the adjective has a short vowel and a single final consonant, double the final consonant. Then add er or est.
    - EXAMPLES:
        - wise   wiser   wisest
        - tiny   tinier   tiniest
        - thin   thinner   thinnest
- To describe one person or thing, use the **positive form**. To compare two people or things, use the **comparative form**. To compare three or more people or things, use the **superlative form**.
    - EXAMPLES:
        - Anita is **tall**.   (positive)
        - Anita is **taller** than Jancy.   (comparative)
        - Anita is the **tallest** of her sisters.   (superlative)

✳ **Write the comparative and superlative forms.**

POSITIVE	COMPARATIVE	SUPERLATIVE
1. smooth	_____	_____
2. busy	_____	_____
3. nice	_____	_____
4. strong	_____	_____
5. easy	_____	_____
6. big	_____	_____
7. kind	_____	_____
8. calm	_____	_____
9. rough	_____	_____
10. narrow	_____	_____
11. brave	_____	_____
12. short	_____	_____
13. happy	_____	_____
14. sad	_____	_____
15. pretty	_____	_____

Language: Usage and Practice HS, SV 1419027867

Name _____ Date _____

Comparing with Other Adjectives

- For most longer adjectives, use <u>more</u> to form the comparative and <u>most</u> to form the superlative.
  - EXAMPLES:
    - Your map was **more helpful** than mine.
    - Your directions were the **most helpful** of all.
- Some adjectives have **irregular comparisons**.
  - EXAMPLES:
    - good better best
    - bad worse worst
- Adjectives can also be compared using <u>less</u> or <u>least</u>.
  - EXAMPLES:
    - Josie is **less patient** than I am.
    - Terry is the **least patient** person I know.

✳ **Write the comparative and superlative forms using <u>more</u> and <u>most</u>.**

POSITIVE	COMPARATIVE	SUPERLATIVE
1. interesting	_____	_____
2. dangerous	_____	_____
3. professional	_____	_____
4. important	_____	_____
5. difficult	_____	_____

✳ **Write the comparative and superlative forms using <u>less</u> and <u>least</u>.**

POSITIVE	COMPARATIVE	SUPERLATIVE
6. helpful	_____	_____
7. practical	_____	_____
8. serious	_____	_____
9. enjoyable	_____	_____
10. beautiful	_____	_____

✳ **Complete each sentence with the comparative or superlative form of the adjective in parentheses. Some are regular adjectives, and some are not.**

11. (rainy) The weather seems _____ this year than last.

12. (faithful) I think dogs are the _____ of all animals.

13. (agreeable) Is Jim _____ than Kent?

14. (busy) Theresa is the _____ person in the office.

15. (long) Which river is _____, the Mississippi or the Amazon?

Language: Usage and Practice HS, SV 1419027867

Name _____ Date _____

Participles

> • A **present participle** or **past participle** is a verb form that may be used as an adjective.
>   EXAMPLES:
>   A **dripping** faucet can be a nuisance.
>   Put the **broken** chair in the **closed** office.

 Underline each participle that is used as an adjective.

1. We saw the <u>injured</u> man when he went to the emergency room.

2. The irritated cab driver sat down beside the waiting travelers.

3. The scampering cat ran to the nearest tree.

4. A team of deep-sea divers discovered the hidden treasure.

5. She is too advanced a tennis player to take beginning lessons.

6. Biting insects swarmed near our construction site.

7. His foot, which was struck by falling glass, was badly injured.

8. The singing group bowed for the clapping guests.

9. The voters heard all of the prepared speeches.

10. The drooping plants perked up after Anna and her watering crew came.

11. The busy host had to seat the waiting customers.

12. The aging truck traveled slowly over the rough road.

13. Everyone ate the melted ice cream and enjoyed it.

14. The moving van will pick up our used furniture.

15. That expanding city will soon be the largest one in the country.

16. Jana pushed open the sliding glass door.

17. Mrs. Wilhelm tried to comfort the terrified boy.

18. The frozen lake looks like a huge reflecting mirror.

19. The commanding officer gave orders to his troops.

20. The painted apartment was ready for the arriving tenants.

21. You need written excuses for extended absences.

22. The grieving widow was happy that her friends were nearby.

23. Keela's growing child needs new clothes for school.

24. The surviving pilot described the accident.

25. The dedicated artist worked slowly on the painting.

26. Homing pigeons were used in the experiment.

27. The whistling youngster trudged slowly down the road.

28. Ironed shirts were stacked neatly at the cleaners.

29. Tom spoke to his troubled friend about the accident.

30. The child ran to his loving father for a comforting hug.

Name _____ Date _____

Adverbs

> - An **adverb** is a word that describes a verb, an adjective, or another adverb.
> - Many adverbs end in <u>ly</u>.
>   EXAMPLES:
>   The rain fell **steadily**.
>   Her absences were **too** frequent.
>   They responded **very quickly**.
> - An adverb usually tells how, when, where, or how often.
>   EXAMPLES:
>   **well** done   **recently** promoted
>   came **here**   **seldom** walked

 Underline the adverbs in each sentence.

1. The secretary read the rules <u>slowly</u> but <u>very</u> <u>clearly</u>.

2. Adam, you are driving too recklessly.

3. The airplane started moving slowly, but it quickly gained speed.

4. I spoke too harshly to my friends.

5. Did the directions help you get there?

6. The report was well written.

7. The man stopped suddenly and quickly turned around.

8. Stacy swallowed her medicine too rapidly.

9. Janice answers the switchboard pleasantly.

10. His little grandson was sleeping soundly.

11. The car was running noisily.

12. The movie was really short, so we returned early.

13. Those trees were severely damaged in the fire.

14. Jackson worked quickly, but steadily, to change the flat tire.

 Write two adverbs to describe each verb. You may want to use a dictionary or a list of adverbs.

15. read   _____   _____

16. think   _____   _____

17. walk   _____   _____

18. eat   _____   _____

19. sing   _____   _____

20. speak   _____   _____

21. drive   _____   _____

22. write   _____   _____

Unit 3: Grammar and Usage
Language: Usage and Practice HS, SV 1419027867

Name _____   Date _____

Adverbs, p. 2

 Underline the adverbs in each sentence.

23. The old car moved <u>slowly</u> up the hill.

24. She answered him very quickly.

25. We arrived at the party too early, so we helped with the decorations.

26. The family waited patiently to hear about the newborn baby.

27. Carina drove the car very cautiously in the snowstorm.

28. Does Marshall always sit here, or may I have this seat?

29. They walked very rapidly in order to get home before the rainstorm.

30. The dog ran swiftly toward its home.

31. Emily quietly waited her turn while others went ahead.

32. We looked everywhere for the missing files.

33. May I leave now, or should I wait for the manager?

34. She drove slowly during the driving test and did well on parallel parking.

35. The nights have been extremely warm, so we go swimming in the evening.

36. He always drives carefully and never runs through yellow lights.

37. Can you swim far under the water without goggles?

38. Come here, and I'll show you a way to sew it neatly.

39. Please work quickly so that we can leave sooner.

40. Deer run very fast at the first sign of danger.

41. I suddenly remembered that I left my jacket in the break room.

42. The snow fell softly on the rooftops of the city.

43. I can write that letter now and mail it there by noon.

44. She wrote too rapidly and made a mistake.

45. Winters there are extremely cold, but summers are very pleasant.

46. Although he was very tired, the clerk spoke politely to the customers.

47. You are reading too rapidly to learn something from it.

48. The team played extremely well.

49. Unfortunately, our machine breaks often.

50. Everyone listened carefully to the doctor's words.

51. We walked slowly in the hot sun.

52. The office workers crossed the street very carefully during the parade.

53. We eagerly watched the parade from the roof of our building.

54. The recreation center was finished recently.

55. We walked everywhere yesterday.

56. My grandmother dearly loves her red hat.

57. I have read this book before.

58. He really wants to learn computer programming.

Name _____ Date _____

Comparing with Adverbs

- An adverb has three forms: **positive**, **comparative**, and **superlative**.
- For one-syllable adverbs and some two-syllable adverbs, add er to form the comparative and est to form the superlative.
  - EXAMPLES:
    - near   nearer   nearest
    - soon   sooner   soonest
- Use the **positive form** to modify without comparing. Use the **comparative form** to compare two actions. Use the **superlative form** to compare three or more actions.
  - EXAMPLES:
    - Katy types **fast**.   (positive)
    - Amy types **faster** than Katy.   (comparative)
    - Edward types the **fastest** of all.   (superlative)
- For all other adverbs, form the comparative with more and the superlative with most.
  - EXAMPLES:
    - Louisa runs **more quickly** than Bob.
    - Greg runs the **most quickly** of all the joggers.

 Underline the word in parentheses that best completes each sentence.

1. Mark arrived (sooner, soonest) than Greg.

2. Todd arrived the (sooner, soonest) of all.

3. They had to work very (hard, harder, hardest).

4. Todd painted (more, most) carefully than Mark.

5. Mark worked (faster, fastest) than Greg, so Mark painted the walls.

6. Lauren worked the (more, most) carefully of all.

 Complete each sentence with the comparative or superlative form of the adverb in parentheses.

7. (soon)   Raymond arrives _____sooner_____ than Juan at morning practice.

8. (fast)   But Juan can run _____ than Raymond.

9. (frequently)   Raymond practices the _____ of all the runners.

10. (quickly)   Today Raymond sprinted _____ than he did yesterday.

11. (seriously)   He is training _____ than Juan.

12. (early)   He even arrives _____ than the coach!

13. (hard)   The coach congratulates Raymond on working the _____ of all.

14. (eagerly)   Raymond does warm-up exercises _____ than a beginner.

15. (fast)   He hopes to run the next race _____ than the last.

Language: Usage and Practice HS, SV 1419027867

Name _____   Date _____

Prepositions

- A **preposition** shows the relationship of a noun or pronoun to another word in the sentence.
  EXAMPLES:
      The young boy ran **into** the house.
      He put his boots **under** the table.
- Here are some commonly used prepositions:

about	above	across	after	against	along	among	around
at	before	behind	below	beside	between	by	down
during	for	from	in	into	near	to	of
on	out	over	through	to	under	until	with

 Underline the prepositions in each sentence.

1. Can you draw a map of your neighborhood for the guests?

2. Go through the first light and around the corner; my house is on the right.

3. I got another package through the mail from Ron.

4. Are you waiting by the bus stop?

5. At the meeting, he spoke to me about your mechanical ability.

6. Our company is ranked among the best; with benefits for its employees, it excels.

7. Her sister Sheena stood beside her.

8. All I want for lunch is a small bowl of vegetable soup with a roll.

9. We went to the house at the end of the street.

10. There were seventy-five post offices in the United States in 1790.

11. Most of the fans stood during the last quarter of the game.

12. I looked for your shoes under the bed, near the TV, and in the closet.

13. We ate dinner at the new restaurant by the river.

14. They stood on the porch and watched for the mail carrier.

15. With any luck, we'll be there between 3:00 and 4:00.

16. We walked down the crowded street against the traffic.

17. Astronaut Sally Ride was the first American woman in space.

18. We went over the report so we could talk to our boss about it.

19. I lost a dime behind the couch, but I found two quarters between the cushions.

20. Before the interview, she sat next to the receptionist in the atrium.

21. There is a bridge across the river in our town.

22. The ball was knocked over the fence and into the pond.

23. After the deadline, we found the old copies of the proposal under the cabinet.

24. The world below the surface of an ocean is strange and beautiful.

25. The rocket headed into space, but it quickly disappeared above the clouds.

26. During the fire drill, employees went out the front door and across the parking lot.

Name _____ Date _____

Prepositional Phrases

> - A **prepositional phrase** is a group of words that begins with a preposition and ends with a noun or pronoun.
>   EXAMPLE: We borrowed some flour **from Karen**.
> - The noun or pronoun in the prepositional phrase is called the **object of the preposition**.
>   EXAMPLE: Melissa hurried **down** the **stairs**.

 Put parentheses around each prepositional phrase. Then underline each preposition and circle the object of the preposition.

1. The airplane was flying (above the clouds).
2. We are moving to a smaller city.
3. Sandra lives on the second block.
4. An old water tower once stood on that hill.
5. The car slid on the wet pavement.
6. Sealing wax was invented in the seventeenth century.
7. I'll take the clock to the repair shop before next week.
8. Tungsten, a metal, was discovered in 1781.
9. Mrs. Griffith knits beautiful sweaters by hand.
10. The ball rolled into the street.
11. Does the animal shelter always keep the puppies in a pen?
12. The children climbed over the fence.
13. She lives in a small apartment on Dover Road.
14. Columbus made three trips to America.
15. Salt Lake City, Utah's capital and largest city, was founded in 1847.
16. Sir Arthur Conan Doyle wrote detective stories about Sherlock Holmes.
17. The library keeps lists of new jobs on the second floor.
18. The geographic center of the United States is in Kansas.
19. The first safety lamp for miners was invented by Sir Humphrey Davy.
20. Many people of North Borneo live in houses that have been built on stilts.
21. The children were charmed by the magician's tricks.
22. We visited the Royal Museum in Ontario.
23. The first automobile show was held in New York City in 1900.
24. We went into the vacant house for a quick look.
25. The first street railway in the world was built in New York in 1832.
26. The inventor of the telephone was born in Scotland.
27. Who is the inventor of the radio?
28. The shadowy outline of the giant skyscrapers was beautiful.
29. Our small boat bobbed in the waves.
30. The swivel chair was invented by Thomas Jefferson.

Name _____   Date _____

Adjective and Adverb Phrases

- In a sentence, a prepositional phrase acts as an adjective or an adverb.
- When the prepositional phrase describes a noun or a pronoun, it is an adjective phrase. It usually tells which one or what kind.

    EXAMPLES: (noun)
      The <u>bird</u> **in the tree** chirped.   (which one)
      The <u>bird</u> **with red wings** flew away.   (what kind)

- When the prepositional phrase modifies a verb, an adjective, or an adverb, it is an adverb phrase. It usually tells how, when, where, or why.

    EXAMPLES: (verb)
      Ted always <u>eats</u> lunch **with coffee**.   (how)
      Ted always <u>eats</u> lunch **after 12:30**.   (when)
      Ted always <u>eats</u> lunch **at the diner**.   (where)
      Ted always <u>eats</u> lunch **for energy**.   (why)

Underline each prepositional phrase. Then write <u>adjective</u> for adjective phrase or <u>adverb</u> for adverb phrase for each prepositional phrase.

_____ 1. They went to the office supply store.

_____ 2. The first savings bank was established in France.

_____ 3. The safety glasses with the broken strap are mine.

_____ 4. Return all books to the public library.

_____ 5. Mr. and Mrs. Skylar live in an old house.

_____ 6. Tim bought a computer with a printer.

_____ 7. Those cans in the trash are recyclable.

_____ 8. Jade is found in Myanmar.

_____ 9. I spent the remainder of my money.

_____ 10. We disagreed over the manager's instructions.

_____ 11. The diameter of a Sequoia tree trunk can reach ten feet.

_____ 12. The capital of New York State is Albany.

_____ 13. The narrowest streets are located near the docks.

_____ 14. Our family went to the movies.

_____ 15. Roald Amundsen reached the South Pole in 1911.

_____ 16. The floor in this room is painted black.

_____ 17. The dead leaves are blowing across the yard.

_____ 18. The blueprints for the new office are displayed in the hall.

_____ 19. The mole's tunnel runs across the lawn.

_____ 20. We finally got home around dark.

Language: Usage and Practice HS, SV 1419027867

Name _____ Date _____

Conjunctions

- A **conjunction** joins words or groups of words.
- A **coordinate conjunction** joins words or groups of words that are related.
- **Correlative conjunctions** are used in pairs to join other words.
  coordinate conjunctions: and   but   nor   or
  correlative conjunctions: either . . . or   neither . . . nor
                                 both . . . and   not only . . . but also

  EXAMPLES:
  Genna is a nurse, **but** Barb is a chef.
  Genna is **not only** a mother **but also** a nurse.

- A **subordinate conjunction** joins groups of words with the main part of a sentence.
  subordinate conjunctions:
  after   although   as   because   before   if
  since   so that   unless   until   when   while
  EXAMPLES:
  When it rains this hard, the roads are slick.
  I'll go to the grocery store **after** the rain stops.

 Underline the coordinate and correlative conjunctions in each sentence.

1. Neither the chairs nor the tables had been dusted.

2. He and I are cousins. We are related not only on my mother's side but also on my father's side of the family.

3. Dawn likes tennis, but Jim prefers running or shooting hoops.

4. We left early, but we missed both the train and the bus.

5. He is not only available but also willing to help.

6. Both hail and rain fell during the storm. It was a dark and dreary day.

7. I have neither time nor energy to waste. My family and my job take all I have.

8. Bowling and tennis are my favorite sports, but I like badminton, too.

9. Either Jan or Dan will bring a portable radio and a flashlight.

 Underline the subordinate conjunction in each sentence.

10. We enjoyed the visit although we were very tired.

11. Although I like to take pictures, I'm not a good photographer.

12. We cannot concentrate if you make so much noise.

13. The party will be over before they get there.

14. Did you see Clarine's baby when she visited the office?

15. Unless you have some objections, I will turn in this report tomorrow.

16. While Justin mowed the lawn, Angie watered the plants.

17. I'll come to see you when you are feeling better.

18. We got here late because we lost the directions.

19. I'm not leaving for home until I file this stack of papers.

     Language: Usage and Practice HS, SV 1419027867

Name _____ Date _____

Using *Their*, *There*, and *They're*

- Their means "belonging to them."
- There means "in that place" or "to that place."
- They're is the contraction for they are.
  EXAMPLES:
  Their baby is sick.
  No one else can get **there** in time.
  They're not going to the movies with us.

 Write their, there, or they're to complete each sentence.

1. Diana and Casey drove _____ their _____ car home from work.

2. Now _____ getting ready to go grocery shopping.

3. _____ neighbor Kwan said he wants to go to the supermarket, too.

4. Diana says they will be glad to take him _____.

5. Casey asks Diana to bring _____ checkbook along.

6. Diana will also call Kwan to tell him when _____ leaving.

7. Kwan says he'll go whenever _____ ready.

8. He offers to help Diana and Casey with _____ shopping.

9. They all want to get _____ before the supermarket gets crowded.

10. When they arrive, they get _____ shopping carts.

11. Then they check _____ grocery lists.

12. Casey is glad _____ so organized about shopping.

13. He likes the supermarket, but he doesn't want to stay _____ very long.

14. Kwan says he doesn't care how long he's _____.

15. Finally, the friends get all of _____ groceries.

16. Diana says _____ ready to go home.

 Underline the correct word in parentheses to complete each sentence.

17. They are over (their, there, they're) standing in front of (their, there, they're) apartment.

18. (Their, There, They're) going to visit (their, there, they're) children in Florida.

19. (Their, There, They're) visiting (their, there, they're) because they have a new grandson.

20. (Their, There, They're) looking forward to (their, there, they're) trip.

21. (Their, There, They're) suitcases are over (their, there, they're) by the car.

Name _____ Date _____

Using *This* or *That* and *These* or *Those*

- Use this and that with singular nouns. Use these and those with plural nouns.
- This and these point to people or things nearby. That and those point to people or things farther away.
    EXAMPLES:
        This movie costs $6.
        That movie was my favorite.
        These people are in line.
        Those latecomers will not get in.
- Them is a pronoun. It is not used with a noun.

 Underline the correct word in parentheses to complete each sentence.

1. Move (those, them) plants inside since it may freeze tonight.

2. (These, That) box in front of me is too heavy to lift.

3. Who brought us (those, them) delicious cookies?

4. Look at (those, them) files. They're a mess.

5. (That, Those) kind of friendship is hard to find.

6. (Those, Them) pictures are beautiful.

7. What are (those, them) sounds I hear?

8. Did you ever meet (those, them) people?

9. We have just developed (these, them) photographs.

10. Do you know any of (those, them) men in computer services?

11. May we take some of (these, them) folders?

12. I have been looking over (these, them) magazines.

13. Do not eat too many of (those, them) hot peppers.

14. I don't like (this, these) kind of cereal.

15. (Those, Them) people should be served next.

16. Stan, please mail (these, them) letters.

17. Look at (those, them) posters I made.

18. (This, That) town is more than fifty miles away.

19. (These, Them) silver coins may be valuable.

20. Look at (those, that) firefighters hustle!

21. Mr. Alphonse, may we look at (these, them) instructions again?

22. We need to return (that, those) library books.

23. (These, Them) clothes need to be washed.

24. Please hand me (that, those) plates.

25. (Those, Them) cookies have nuts in them.

26. Will you fix the flat tire on (this, these) van?

27. (This, these) group of people is standing in line to see (that, those) play.

Language: Usage and Practice HS, SV 1419027867

Using *Affect* or *Effect* and *Accept* or *Except*

- Affect means "to produce a change in" or "to influence."
- Effect means "the result."
  - EXAMPLES:
    - Poor soil may **affect** the plants.
    - We won't know the **effect** until the plants come up.
- Accept means "to take what is offered or given" or "to receive."
- Except means "left out" or "excluding."
  - EXAMPLES:
    - Please **accept** the invitation to my party.
    - I invited everyone to the party **except** Dee.

✺ **Complete each sentence by writing the correct word in parentheses.**

1. (affects, effects)   The dry, parched soil showed the _____effects_____ of the long drought.

2. (affected, effected)   The orange trees were _____ by the lack of moisture.

3. (affect, effect)   The drought will _____ the orange crop this year.

4. (affect, effect)   The Agriculture Department studies the _____ of the drought.

5. (affected, effected)   Unusually cold weather has also _____ crops this year.

6. (affects, effects)   No one knows what the long-term _____ will be.

✺ **Complete each sentence by writing the correct word in parentheses.**

7. (accept, except)   Will Mrs. Kern _____accept_____ my reason for missing the appointment?

8. (accept, except)   (accept, except)   She will usually _____ any explanation,

   _____ one that sounds ridiculous.

9. (accept, except)   Mei was going to show us how to cook a special noodle dish,

   _____ she forgot to bring the recipe to cooking class.

10. (accept, except)   I like all fruit _____ bananas.

11. (accepted, excepted)   Sylvia _____ her supervisor's decision about the promotion.

✺ **Write sentences using each of these four words: affect, effect, accept, and except.**

_____

_____

_____

_____

Language: Usage and Practice HS, SV 1419027867

Double Negatives

> - The words <u>no</u>, <u>not</u>, <u>never</u>, <u>hardly</u>, <u>scarcely</u>, <u>seldom</u>, <u>none</u>, and <u>nothing</u> are **negatives**.
> - If you use two negatives, you create a **double negative**. One negative word cancels the other.
>
>   EXAMPLES:
>
>   There **wasn't anything** left to do.   (correct)
>   There **wasn't nothing** left to do.   (incorrect)

 Underline the correct word in parentheses to complete each sentence.

1. We couldn't see (anything, nothing) through the fog.

2. The warehouse manager didn't know (anything, nothing) about the delay.

3. I know (any, none) of the people on this bus.

4. Rosa couldn't do (anything, nothing) about changing the time for our training.

5. We didn't have (any, no) printed programs.

6. I don't want (any, no) cereal for breakfast this morning.

7. Please don't speak to (anyone, no one) about the surprise party.

8. There isn't (any, no) ink in this pen.

9. Didn't you make (any, no) copies for the other people?

10. I have had (any, no) time to repair the lawn mower.

11. She hasn't said (anything, nothing) about her accident.

12. Hardly (anything, nothing) pleases him.

13. There aren't (any, no) pears in this supermarket.

14. There aren't (any, no) newspapers left at the store.

15. There was (anybody, nobody) in the house.

16. He doesn't have (any, no) idea why the fax machine isn't working.

17. I haven't done (any, none) of the work I had planned to do today.

18. I hope I haven't done (anything, nothing) to offend Greg.

19. We don't have (any, no) water pressure.

20. There wasn't (any, no) reason that I know of that the mail was late.

21. They could hear (anything, nothing) because of the airplane's noise.

22. The salesperson didn't have (any, no) samples on display.

23. I have (any, no) money with me.

24. Hasn't he cooked (any, none) of the spaghetti?

25. We haven't (any, no) more packages to wrap.

26. Wasn't there (anyone, no one) at home?

27. My dog has never harmed (anybody, nobody).

28. They seldom have (anyone, no one) absent from their meetings.

29. There weren't (any, no) clouds in the sky.

Name _____ Date _____

Troublesome Words

- Some words are confused because they look and sound similar. Check to make sure you spell the word you mean to use correctly.

    advise and **advice**

    Advise is a verb, and advice is a noun.
    EXAMPLES:
    Ben should do what his doctors **advise**.
    Ben should listen to his doctors' **advice**.

    loose and **lose**

    Loose is an adjective that means "free" or "not close together."
    Lose is a verb that means "to misplace" or "to have loss."
    EXAMPLES:
    Your shoelace is too **loose**.
    Don't **lose** your shoes!

    past and **passed**

    Past refers to time before the present.
    Passed is the past tense of the verb pass.
    EXAMPLES:
    She got the job because of her **past** experience.
    We **passed** each other on the street.

    plane and **plain**

    Plane means "a flat or level surface," "a tool," or "an airplane."
    Plain means "not fancy" or "a flat area of land."
    EXAMPLES:
    Did you travel by **plane**?
    Tanya ordered a **plain** hamburger.

    quiet and **quite**

    Quiet means "silent" or "still."
    Quite means "to a great extent" or "completely."
    EXAMPLES:
    The library is supposed to be a **quiet** place.
    Reynaldo is **quite** lucky.

 Complete each sentence by writing the correct word in parentheses.

1. (plane, plain)   Manuel bought a ____plain____ blue sweater.

2. (advise, advice)   Sara never listened to Mina's _____.

3. (past, passed)   People study history to learn from the _____.

4. (quiet, quite)   There is _____ a difference between the cost of airplane and bus tickets.

5. (past, passed)   Mauricio _____ the parade on his way home from work.

6. (lose, loose)   If you accidentally _____ your driver's license, report it immediately.

7. (quiet, quite)   The speaker asked for _____ before she began to speak.

8. (plane, plain)   If you miss this _____, you can't get home until tomorrow morning.

9. (advise, advice)   Would you please _____ me on the best buy in computers?

10. (past, passed)   The time had already _____ for him to submit his application.

11. (lose, loose)   The chimp broke out of its cage and was on the _____ in the zoo.

12. (plane, plain)   Do you know how to use a _____ for woodworking?

13. (lose, loose)   I often _____ the change out of my pocket.

Name _____ Date _____

Unit 3 Test

Underline each noun. Then write C above each common noun and P above each proper noun.

1. Honolulu is the chief city and capital of Hawaii.

2. Rainbow Natural Bridge is hidden away in southern Utah.

3. Igor Stravinsky was a well-known composer from Russia.

4. Jean asked her niece to visit after Thanksgiving.

Complete each sentence with the plural form of the word in parentheses.

5. (woman) The _____ in the choir are rehearsing tonight.

6. (foot) I stood on my _____ too long baking cookies.

7. (porch) I like old Victorian homes with enclosed _____.

8. (sister-in-law) Gina has three _____.

Complete each sentence with the possessive form of the noun in parentheses.

9. (children) Hector took his son to the _____ store to buy new clothes.

10. (lawyers) Ms. Esposito is attending a _____ conference.

11. (candidate) Did you hear that _____ most recent speech?

Underline the verb in each sentence. Write A before each sentence with an action verb and L before each sentence with a linking verb.

_____12. The car reached the narrow bridge.

_____13. Brush your teeth frequently.

_____14. Which driver won the race?

_____15. Donna was first on the list.

_____16. Mrs. Strauss seems anxious.

_____17. This newspaper is the early edition.

Underline the verb phrase in each sentence. Then circle the helping verb or verbs.

18. I should have remembered his birthday.

19. Tom is designing a newsletter for our company.

20. Did you mop the floor?

21. Your package might not arrive this week.

22. Lucy and I have opened the package.

23. Dave should not have washed the car.

Unit 3 Test, p. 2

Underline the correct pronoun or pronouns in each sentence.

24. Miss Matson spoke to Jennifer and (I, me) about it.

25. Stan and Tom bought (they, themselves) some new shirts.

26. Please bring Anne and (I, me) some clean towels.

27. Here comes (my, me) brother David.

28. (He, Him) and Susan were late today.

Underline each adjective. Circle each adverb.

29. This small coat fit me comfortably last year.

30. The large cabinet was completely filled with cleaning supplies.

31. I slept soundly until the howling dogs awoke me.

32. The best runners ran easily to the finish line.

33. A new family recently moved into the gray house.

Put parentheses around each prepositional phrase. Then underline each preposition and circle the object of the preposition.

34. Put this basket of clothes in the laundry.

35. Jacob installed the plumbing at a new restaurant near the river.

36. The top of the mountain is usually covered with snow.

37. The house on the corner was sold in one week.

38. Did you come to the office with your family during your vacation?

Identify the part of speech of each underlined word. Darken the circle by your answer.

39. The police officer walked <u>across</u> the street.
- Ⓐ adverb
- Ⓑ conjunction
- Ⓒ preposition
- Ⓓ pronoun

40. That was such a <u>pleasant</u> surprise.
- Ⓐ adverb
- Ⓑ adjective
- Ⓒ pronoun
- Ⓓ preposition

41. Dark clouds <u>slowly</u> gathered in the north.
- Ⓐ conjunction
- Ⓑ pronoun
- Ⓒ adjective
- Ⓓ adverb

42. Would you like to see the photographs that we took on <u>our</u> trip?
- Ⓐ pronoun
- Ⓑ adjective
- Ⓒ adverb
- Ⓓ noun

43. <u>Someone</u> called me and woke me up.
- Ⓐ adverb
- Ⓑ pronoun
- Ⓒ preposition
- Ⓓ adjective

44. Gina and her friends went to the <u>new</u> mall today.
- Ⓐ conjunction
- Ⓑ adverb
- Ⓒ preposition
- Ⓓ adjective

Name _____ Date _____

Using Capital Letters

- Capitalize the first word of a sentence and of each line of poetry.
    EXAMPLES: Sharon wrote a poem. It began as follows:
        One cold and starry night
        We saw the night birds taking flight.
- Capitalize the first word of a quotation.
    EXAMPLE: Ms. Barnes said, "Everyone should learn a poem."
- Capitalize the first, last, and all important words in the titles of books, chapters, poems, stories, songs, plays, movies, magazines, TV shows, newspapers, and works of art.
    EXAMPLES: "The Necklace"; The Call of the Wild; Wheel of Fortune; Newsweek
- Capitalize all proper nouns.
    EXAMPLES: Lanelle Smith; Aunt Joann, Main Street, Africa, Minnesota, Rocky Mountains, New Year's Day, August, Kennedy High School, Sea Voyager
- Capitalize all proper adjectives. A proper adjective is an adjective that is made from a proper noun.
    EXAMPLES: the French language, Chinese food, Japanese tourists
- Capitalize the pronoun I and all contractions with I.
    EXAMPLES: I, I'm, I'll, I've, I'd

 Circle each letter that should be capitalized. Write the capital letter above it.

1. once i heard someone say, "poems can be beautiful, sad, exciting, or funny."

2. do you know who wrote "the charge of the light brigade"?

3. The british ship *titanic* sank on its first trip from england to the united states.

4. The missouri river flows through pierre, south dakota.

5. "what time does the game start?" asked darrell.

6. as he turned on the TV, dave said, "the tonight show is my favorite program."

7. the first law course offered by an american college was taught by george wythe.

8. he taught many famous people, including thomas jefferson and james monroe.

9. the song "the battle hymn of the republic" was written by julia ward howe.

10. that movie i missed, a league of their own, is on television tonight.

11. he asked, "have you ever seen hoover dam?"

12. we ate at a german restaurant in new ulm, texas.

13. sequoia national park is on the western slope of the sierra nevada mountains in california.

14. i like a play by william shakespeare called romeo and juliet.

Name _____ Date _____

Using Capital Letters, p. 2

- Capitalize a person's title when it comes before a name.
  EXAMPLES: Doctor Spock, Judge Douglas, Governor Long
- Capitalize initials and abbreviations of titles.
  EXAMPLES: Mr. J. D. Biggs, Dr. Chang, Pres. Roosevelt
- Capitalize abbreviations of days and months, parts of addresses, and titles of members of the armed forces.
- Also capitalize all letters in the abbreviations of states.
  EXAMPLES: Sat.; Nov.; 67 S. Sherman St.; Col. Fernando Garza; Mobile, AL
- Capitalize the names of specific products, companies, stores, schools, organizations, and teams.
  EXAMPLES: Yummy Lemon Drops; Parson Industries; Shoppers World; Stanford University; American Cancer Society; New York Giants

 Circle each letter that should be capitalized. Write the capital letter above it.

15. mayor myer and senator snivley had an important meeting friday night.

16. dr. wolf is a veterinarian at the local animal hospital.

17. The application said to contact ms. lenore lindley.

18. We received a special letter from judge randolph.

19. We were upset that gov. luzer signed the legislation.

20. The legislation was proposed by mrs. carol creepton.

21. The speaker at the assembly will be supt. adams.

22. Will mr. olden be the new history instructor?

23. The chicago white sox won the world series in 2005.

24. Their opponents were the houston astros.

25. When is maj. stryker expected back from his tour overseas?

26. The big sale is at 701 s. carson st.

27. Have you ever been to phoenix, az?

28. There is a house for sale at the corner of oak ave. and water st.

29. The letter from memphis, tn, took only two days to arrive.

30. Did you know that col. clink will be stationed in dover, nh?

31. His address will be 1234 bentley boulevard, dover, nh 03805.

32. They work at mason manufacturing and make mason's mighty mothballs.

Language: Usage and Practice HS, SV 1419027867

Using Commas

- Use a **comma** between words or groups of words that are in a series. With only two items, don't use a comma.
  - EXAMPLE: Colorado, Snake, Ohio, Mississippi, and Missouri are names of well-known American rivers.
- Use a comma before a conjunction in a compound sentence.
  - EXAMPLE: The rivers were once used mainly for transportation, but now they are used for industry and recreation.
- Use a comma after a subordinate clause when it begins a sentence.
  - EXAMPLE: When I got home, the door was locked.

 Add commas where needed in the sentences below.

1. The United States exports cotton corn and wheat to many countries.

2. The children played softball ran races and splashed in the pool.

3. Larry held the nail securely but he couldn't hit it squarely on the head.

4. The report to the committee was clear accurate and concise.

5. Mike fixed the roof and Roger replaced the windows.

6. Alex Frank Candace and Jim go to the gym each day.

7. The rain fell steadily and the lightning flashed.

8. Gloves goggles and helmets are important pieces of safety equipment.

9. Alan Carri and Chet will arrive first so they can start the project.

10. Our new apartment must be cleaned painted and repaired.

11. Jerome should stop running or he will be out of breath.

12. Walking running and biking are all good exercise.

13. Aaron will cook dinner or he will take us out to eat.

14. Mindy enjoyed the corn but Frank liked the green beans.

15. My car has a dead battery a broken starter or old spark plugs.

16. I didn't tell your secret to anyone but Sara probably did.

17. This job requires typing filing and shorthand and I'm not sure I can do it all.

18. Suzi peeled the peaches and Victor sliced them.

19. Jason reminded me to pack warm socks sweaters and gloves.

20. Baseball is Leo's favorite sport but Della prefers soccer.

21. Kent must fill out an application or he won't get an interview.

22. We have puzzles games and toys for the children.

Name _____ Date _____

Using Commas, p. 2

- Use a comma to set off a quotation from the rest of the sentence.
  - EXAMPLES: "We should leave early," said Taylor.
  - Taylor said, "We should leave early."
- Use two commas to set off a divided quotation. Do not capitalize the first word of the second part of the quotation.
  - EXAMPLE: "We should leave early," Taylor said, "or we'll be stuck in traffic."
- Use a comma to set off the name of a person who is being addressed.
  - EXAMPLE: Kayla, would you like to leave now?
- Use a comma to set off words like <u>yes</u>, <u>no</u>, <u>well</u>, <u>oh</u>, <u>first</u>, <u>next</u>, and <u>finally</u> at the beginning of a sentence.
  - EXAMPLE: Well, I guess so.
- Use a comma to set off an appositive.
  - EXAMPLE: Kaitlin, Kayla's sister, is a dentist in Sacramento.

 Add commas where needed in the sentences below.

23. Diana a worker at the shoe store talked to Justin her boss.

24. "Justin when should I open the store for the sale" she asked.

25. "Oh you should open a little before 9:00" Justin said.

26. "I can come in earlier" said Diana "if you want me to open up earlier."

27. "Yes that's a good idea" Justin said "so we can arrange sale signs before we open."

28. "I'll see you in the morning Justin and I'll be ready for the crowd" she said as she left.

29. Dr. Anderson a dietitian is an expert on proper eating.

30. "First it's important to eat a well-balanced diet" he said.

31. "Yes but how do we know what the best foods are?" asked a student.

32. "Well you need to study your eating habits" said Dr. Anderson.

33. "Next you should keep a journal of the foods you eat" he said.

34. "Dr. Anderson what do you mean by the right size of servings?" asked Pierce.

35. "OK that's a good question" he said.

36. "A serving Pierce is a certain amount of a food" said Dr. Anderson.

37. "For example an athlete will need more calories than a less active student" explained Dr. Anderson.

38. "Class remember to eat foods from each basic food group" he said.

39. Carlton my nephew lives in that old house near the river.

40. Joe Montana a famous quarterback talked about the football game.

Language: Usage and Practice HS, SV 1419027867

Quotation Marks

- Use **quotation marks** to enclose the exact words of a speaker.
- Capitalize the first word of the beginning of a quotation and use a comma to separate it from the rest of a sentence.
    - EXAMPLE: **"I'm really hungry,"** Neena complained.
- A quotation may come at the beginning or end of a sentence, and it may be divided.
- Put periods and commas inside the closing quotation marks.
    - EXAMPLES: Neena said, **"I wish we could eat dinner now."**
    - **"If that's what you'd like,"** Dad replied, **"let's eat."**
- If the quotation is a question or an exclamation, put the correct punctuation inside the quotation marks.
- But if the whole sentence is a question, put the question mark outside the quotation marks.
    - EXAMPLES: **"Will you set the table?"** Dad asked.
    - **"You bet!"** Neena shouted.
    - Did I surprise you when I said, **"Let's eat"**?

 Each sentence contains a quotation. Put quotation marks where they belong to enclose each quotation.

1. "Miss Alton, have you read this magazine article on getting your GED?" Karl asked.

2. I'd like your opinion of what the article suggests, Karl added.

3. Shannon, have you ever been to Rock Springs? asked Dylan.

4. It's a great place for a picnic, Dylan said, and it has a pool nearby.

5. Uncle Daniel, have you ever baked an apple pie? Chad asked.

6. Stella, how many members of the club are in this county? asked Manuel.

7. There are sixty active members, replied Stella.

8. I have been saving money since I started keeping a budget, said Elena.

9. Ava, I brought you a great book, Eddie said.

10. We will learn to do spreadsheets next week, said Mr. Andrews.

11. I'm going to plant the spinach just as soon as I get home, said Dee.

12. When do we start on our mountain trip? inquired Ernesto.

13. You don't know, said our guest, how happy I am to be in your house.

14. My sister, said Jenny, brought these beautiful baskets from El Paso.

15. We will go to the park for a picnic, said Sandra.

16. Will you carry this package for me? asked Helena.

17. Did he surprise you when he said, You can go home early ?

18. Where is the nearest cafe? inquired the stranger.

19. Where are you going, Max? asked his assistant.

20. Stay right here, said Walt, and I'll bring you the form you need.

21. Guess who got the job, said Lorna.

22. We have to get up early, said Ben, if we want to see the sunrise.

Quotation Marks, p. 2

> - Use quotation marks to enclose titles of these short works:
>   poems   songs   articles   short stories   chapters of books
>   EXAMPLES: The magazine article is called **"Working From Home."**
>   **"Where Have All the Flowers Gone"** is a folk song.
>   Read Chapter 16, **"Using the Computer Mouse."**
> - Use quotation marks to enclose exact words from written sources.
> - Use quotation marks to enclose expressions.
>   EXAMPLES: The reviewer wrote, **"an action movie with heart."**
>   **"Boot up"** doesn't mean to kick your computer.

✻ **Check the punctuation in each sentence. Write C for correct punctuation or I for incorrect punctuation.**

___I___ **23.** After you read "Chapter 4, Going Nowhere," skip to "Chapter 18, Another Journey."

_____ **24.** The song Kay's daughter learned in preschool is "On Top of Old Smoky."

_____ **25.** "Watch out! This is a hard hat area," warned the supervisor.

_____ **26.** "Steve, are you afraid," she asked?

_____ **27.** My poem is called If You Can.

_____ **28.** What do you mean when you say, "Never say never"?

_____ **29.** Amy told me "you shouldn't have been concerned".

_____ **30.** "Emily," she said, "let's meet at the restaurant after work, OK?"

_____ **31.** Do you like the old Irish song called "Danny Boy?"

_____ **32.** I'm a real fan of Dolly Parton and "I Will Always Love You."

_____ **33.** "Have you read that computer book yet," Sheila asked her friend?

_____ **34.** I read the chapter on saving files, "How to Save Your Work."

✻ **Add quotation marks and other punctuation marks where they are needed.**

35. Kim seems really distracted today I said to Luisa.

36. I know exclaimed Luisa it's as if she's not hearing anything I say.

37. I wonder if something is wrong, I said, or do you think she's thinking about the horror movie we saw last night?

38. I don't know if we can blame it on the movie, Luisa said, laughing, but I do know she's been singing that song from the movie all day!

39. Did you hear her, too asked Luisa

40. Yes I said and I started singing the song myself!

41. I played football with my kids all weekend said Dave.

42. So, did Jason make the team this year? asked Karla.

43. Yes, he did said Dave and he can't wait for their first game.

44. But I'm so sore I can hardly move today Dave added.

45. Have you ever heard the expression You're only as young as you feel?

Name _____ Date _____

Apostrophes

- Use an **apostrophe** in a contraction to show where a letter or letters have been taken out.
  EXAMPLES: **I'm** too tired to finish.   I am too tired to finish.
            I **can't** work any faster.   I can not work any faster.
- Use an apostrophe to form a possessive noun.
- Add apostrophe and s to most singular nouns, even if the noun ends in s.
- Add only an apostrophe to most plural nouns.
- Add an apostrophe and s to nouns with irregular plurals.
  EXAMPLES: **Maria's** sons are all musicians.   (singular)
            Mr. Williams's sons are drummers.   (singular)
            All of their **sons'** instruments are new.   (plural)
            Their **children's** band is very popular.   (plural)

 Write the words in each sentence that should have an apostrophe. Place apostrophes where they are needed.

1. I cant make it to the homeowners meeting.   _____can't_____   ____homeowners'____

2. I cant go until Seths project is completed.   _____   _____

3. Youll need two days notice to finish this report.   _____   _____

4. Ive heard that Jeffs report was excellent.   _____   _____

5. Isnt that one of Cole Porters songs?   _____   _____

6. Kate, didnt you want Sues job?   _____   _____

7. Havent you seen Pauls apartment?   _____   _____

8. Jim didnt fall off the workmans ladder.   _____   _____

9. The employees paychecks didnt arrive on time.   _____   _____

10. The police officers uniforms arent ready.   _____   _____

11. I hope the dog isnt chewing the babys shoe.   _____   _____

12. Julio isnt going to the companys sales meeting.   _____   _____

13. Carlas house wasnt painted until last week.   _____   _____

14. The captains ship was one of the navys newest.   _____   _____

15. The phone companys system wasnt installed yet.   _____   _____

16. Mens coats are sold in Shannons new store.   _____   _____

17. The womens basketball game hasnt been cancelled.   _____   _____

18. There arent enough copies of Anns memo for us all.   _____   _____

www.harcourtschoolsupply.com
© Harcourt Achieve Inc. All rights reserved.

102

Unit 4: Capitalization and Punctuation
Language: Usage and Practice HS, SV 1419027867

Name _____ Date _____

Semicolons

> - Use a **semicolon** to join two closely related sentences.
> - Two simple sentences joined with a semicolon become a compound sentence.
>   EXAMPLES: **two simple sentences:**
>   Ivan spent his vacation in Maine. He enjoys fishing there.
>   **compound sentence with semicolon:**
>   Ivan spent his vacation in Maine; he enjoys fishing there.
> - Compound sentences may also contain words such as <u>for example</u>, <u>besides</u>, <u>consequently</u>, <u>however</u>, <u>nevertheless</u>, <u>instead</u>, <u>otherwise</u>, or <u>therefore</u>. Use semicolons before and commas after these words.
>   EXAMPLES: **compound sentences with introductory words:**
>   Pete didn't see the movie; **instead**, he wrote a letter.
>   Ian is from London; **however**, he's lived here longer.

 Add semicolons and commas where they are needed in each compound sentence.

1. Claire enjoys babysitting for neighbors; however, she also likes working on her car.

2. Claire is a big fan of educational TV for example she watches the auto repair show.

3. Claire changed the oil in her car and checked the tires then she washed the car.

4. Claire's friends ask her about basic car maintenance they know nothing about cars.

5. Claire doesn't think she knows enough nevertheless she usually agrees to help.

6. Vicky was always asking for help as a result she wanted to pay Claire for her time.

7. Claire was embarrassed she didn't want to accept money.

8. Finally, Vicky talked her into accepting money it helped pay Claire's bills.

 Check the punctuation in each sentence. Write <u>C</u> for correct punctuation or <u>I</u> for incorrect punctuation.

____C____ 9. David likes to make model soldiers; his models are extremely accurate and very detailed.

_____ 10. He learns about a time period first; otherwise, he might add wrong details to his soldiers.

_____ 11. To begin, he decides on the kind of soldier; and determines which kit he'd like to buy.

_____ 12. Even though he uses a kit; his soldiers never look exactly like the kits do.

_____ 13. He constructs the figures using the directions; however, he adds his own special details.

_____ 14. He uses things around the house; for example, he uses bits of metal, wood, and fabric.

_____ 15. Sometimes David uses leftover plastic; he melts pieces and shapes them into tools.

_____ 16. Once I saw him crawl under his car, he was trying to match the color of road dirt.

_____ 17. A miniature Napoleon sits on his mantle; he's short, but he wears real plumes on his hat.

Write two simple sentences that you could put together in a compound sentence. Then use a semicolon to join them.

18. _____

_____

Language: Usage and Practice HS, SV 1419027867

Name _____ Date _____

Colons

> • Use a **colon** after the greeting in a business letter.
>   EXAMPLES: Dear Mrs. Jones: Dear Sirs:
> • Use a colon between the hour and the minute to write the time.
>   EXAMPLES: 1:30 P.M.   6:15 A.M.   11:47
> • Use a colon to introduce a list.
>   EXAMPLE: The supply list includes these items: pens, pencils, note pads,
>   tape, staples, and erasers.
> • Use a colon to call attention to something that will follow.
>   EXAMPLES: Important: The meeting starts at 1:00 P.M. sharp.
>   Note: That rule doesn't apply to this section.

 Add colons where they are needed in each sentence.

1. At 2:10 this afternoon, the meeting will start.

2. Please bring these materials employee handbook, schedule, red pen, and highlighter.

3. The meeting should be over by 4 30.

4. Notice This will be the last orientation meeting this month.

5. We will discuss rules of conduct at 3 00 and have a short question period.

 Add colons where they are needed in the business letter.

6. September 3, 2007

7. Ms. Meredith Thompson

   Customer Relations Supervisor

   Tony's Toy Company

   872 North Airport Blvd., Suite 100

   Portland, Oregon 98757

8. Dear Ms. Thompson

9. I am writing to express my concern over a toy I bought from your company last week.
    The label on the box says the package contains the following items one doll, one ink
    pad, three stamps, and four sheets of decals. The package I brought home contained
    only these items one doll and two sheets of decals.

10. When I realized the problem, I called the store where I bought the toy at approximately
     10 00 A.M. that morning. The store manager told me I had two choices Return the toy
     for a full refund or keep it and stop complaining!

11. Please note This is not an acceptable solution. I want to exchange the toy for a new
     one with all the correct pieces. I look forward to hearing from you. Thank you very much.

12. Sincerely,

    Mia Kaplan

Unit 4: Capitalization and Punctuation
                                                                  Language: Usage and Practice HS, SV 1419027867

Name _____ Date _____

Hyphens and Dashes

- Use a **hyphen** in some compound words between the smaller words.
    - EXAMPLES: sister-in-law   middle-aged man   old-fashioned girl
    - great-grandfather   two-story home   well-behaved child
- Use a hyphen in compound numbers from 21 to 99.
    - EXAMPLES: twenty-one   sixty-sixth   ninety-nine
- Use a hyphen to divide a word that comes at the end of a line.
    - EXAMPLE: When the governor finishes his speech, the re-
    - porters will be able to ask their questions.
- Use a dash in a sentence to show an abrupt break in thought.
    - EXAMPLE: Katy Parks—we call her "Space Cadet"—is the new cashier.

 Add hyphens where they are needed in each sentence.

1. Only fifty-one employees applied to take classes after work.

2. The entire customer service department will take computer classes.

3. A computer software expert will give the classes.

4. The sign up sheet will be posted in the employee lounge.

5. Ms. Chambers will talk about new computers for the twenty first century.

6. The corner bookstore has seventy five copies of the computer manual.

7. The manual is a well written book, but the classes will be helpful, too.

8. The vice presidents of several large companies recommend the course.

9. In fact, they call it an A plus class for user friendly companies.

 On each line, copy the word and insert a hyphen to show where to divide the word if it came at the end of a line. Use a dictionary and look for dots between syllables to divide the words.

10. compute ___com-pute_____   14. enclose _____

11. suppose _____   15. frighten _____

12. labor _____   16. outside _____

13. hyphen _____   17. corner _____

 Insert dashes where they are needed in the sentences below.

18. Suddenly—and don't ask me how—the locked door swung open.

19. Maria Maria Reyna, I mean went to find out what happened.

20. She walked towards the door she was really trembling and peered outside.

21. Maria the whole group of us, for that matter saw nothing unusual.

22. We never found out even though we tested the lock why the door blew open.

23. Some things we learned since that incident just can't be explained logically.

Name _____ Date _____

Unit 4 Test

Check the capitalization in each sentence. Write C for correct capitalization or I for incorrect capitalization.

_____ **1.** Last august we visited the state of Oregon in the Pacific Northwest.

_____ **2.** Joseph's apartment is on Michigan Avenue, on the north side of the street.

_____ **3.** Is antarctica a continent?

_____ **4.** Many centuries ago, Vikings lived in what is now norway, sweden, and denmark.

_____ **5.** Do Rosa and her sister live on north remington street?

_____ **6.** Egypt is located in the northern part of Africa.

Choose the item in each group that has correct capitalization. Darken the circle by your choice.

7. Ⓐ A handbook of grammar
   Ⓑ A Handbook Of Grammar
   Ⓒ A handbook of Grammar
   Ⓓ A Handbook of Grammar

8. Ⓐ Bank of Credit in New york city
   Ⓑ Bank of Credit in New York City
   Ⓒ bank Of Credit In New York City
   Ⓓ bank of credit In New York City

9. Ⓐ spike Lee's do the right Thing
   Ⓑ Spike lee's Do The Right Thing
   Ⓒ Spike Lee's do The Right Thing
   Ⓓ Spike Lee's Do the Right Thing

10. Ⓐ "Trees," By joyce Kilmer
   Ⓑ "trees," by Joyce kilmer
   Ⓒ "Trees," by Joyce Kilmer
   Ⓓ "Trees," By Joyce kilmer

11. Ⓐ Dallas Cowboys vs. buffalo Bills
   Ⓑ Dallas Cowboys vs. Buffalo Bills
   Ⓒ Dallas Cowboys vs. Buffalo bills
   Ⓓ Dallas cowboys vs. Buffalo bills

12. Ⓐ Joe's uncle from Iowa, Uncle Max
   Ⓑ Joe's Uncle from Iowa, uncle Max
   Ⓒ Joe's uncle from iowa, uncle Max
   Ⓓ joe's uncle from Iowa, uncle Max

Circle each letter that should be capitalized. Write the capital letter above it.

13. capt. margaret k. hansen

2075 lakeview st.

phoenix, az 85072

14. jackson school Track Meet

at wilson stadium

tues., sept. 26, 10:30

15. gary l. louis, m.d.

5931 congress rd.

syracuse, ny 13217

16. thanksgiving Concert

wed., nov. 23, 11:00

See ms. evans for details.

Unit 4 Test, p. 2

Check how the commas, semicolons, and quotation marks are used in each sentence.
Write C for correct punctuation or I for incorrect punctuation.

_____ **17.** If you have ever been bowling; you know how hard it is to get a strike.

_____ **18.** Do you think Leon, the best bowler in the league will bowl tonight?

_____ **19.** After taking lessons, I am a better bowler.

_____ **20.** I'm a better bowler, but I'm still not a very good bowler.

_____ **21.** Bowling is a game of skill; therefore, practice is important.

Add commas, semicolons, and quotation marks where they are needed.

22. Frank said Medicine helps to heal our bodies music helps to heal our souls.

23. Cats have highly sensitive whiskers consequently they can become agitated when something brushes against their face.

24. The label on the sweater told where the sweater was made it read Made in USA.

25. I'm certain she was born in Paris Texas not Paris France but let's call her to be sure.

26. Marcus did not begin the graphics class this semester instead he took a painting class.

Read each sentence and decide what capitalization and punctuation are needed.
Darken the circle by your answer.

27. Morris likes the following animals for pets cats dogs birds and fish

Ⓐ Morris likes the following animals for pets; cats, dogs birds and fish.

Ⓑ Morris likes the following animals for pets: cats, dogs, birds, and fish.

Ⓒ Morris likes the—following animals for pets— cats, dogs, birds, and fish.

28. Although david left a little late he did get to the party on time

Ⓐ Although david left a little late: he did get to the party on time.

Ⓑ Although David left a little late. He did get to the party on time.

Ⓒ Although David left a little late, he did get to the party on time.

29. Its time for lunch not breakfast

Ⓐ It's time for lunch, not breakfast.

Ⓑ Its time for lunch, not breakfast.

Ⓒ It's time, for lunch, not breakfast.

30. Have you read the article, how to have a successful interview

Ⓐ Have you read the article "How to Have a Successful Interview"?

Ⓑ Have you read the article, How To Have A Successful Interview.

Ⓒ Have you read the article "How to Have a Successful Interview?"

31. The delgados live at 4367 n evergreen st tacoma washington

Ⓐ The Delgados live at 4367 n. Evergreen st., Tacoma Washington

Ⓑ The Delgados live at 4367 N. Evergreen St., Tacoma, Washington.

Ⓒ The delgados live at 4367 N. Evergreen St. Tacoma Washington.

32. Lola yelled watch out for the candle on the table

Ⓐ Lola yelled, "Watch out for the candle on the table!"

Ⓑ Lola yelled! Watch out for the candle on the table.

Ⓒ Lola yelled, "watch out for the candle on the table."

Topic Sentences

- A **topic sentence** states the **main idea** or topic of a paragraph. It tells the reader what the paragraph is about.
- Other sentences in the paragraph tell more about the topic and support the main idea. They give specific information about the topic.
- A topic sentence is often the first sentence in the paragraph. But a topic sentence can be at the beginning, middle, or end of the paragraph.

  EXAMPLES:

  Be prepared before you buy a used car. Know how much the car is worth and how much you are able to pay. Make a list of questions you want to ask about the car. Inspect the car yourself, or have a trusted mechanic do it for you. Finally, if possible, talk with the person who actually owned the car.

  "Oh, no," she said aloud as she drove alone down the narrow, moonlit street. "I knew I should've taken that first exit off the freeway," she thought to herself. But it was too late now. She had forgotten to get directions to the restaurant from Manuel. **Alicia was lost, and she was going to be late for her own birthday party.**

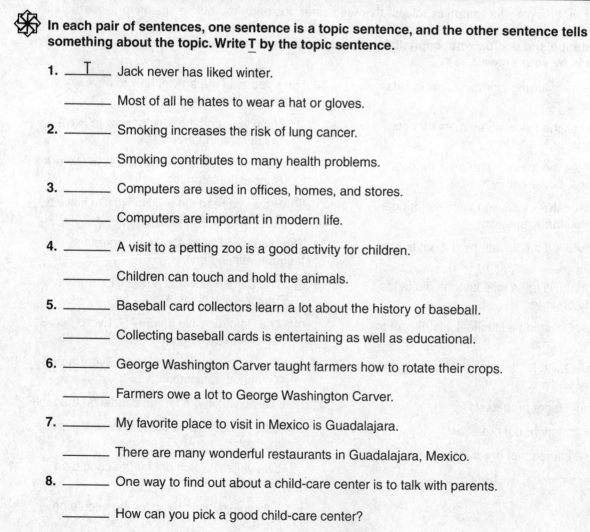

In each pair of sentences, one sentence is a topic sentence, and the other sentence tells something about the topic. Write T by the topic sentence.

1. __T__ Jack never has liked winter.

   _____ Most of all he hates to wear a hat or gloves.

2. _____ Smoking increases the risk of lung cancer.

   _____ Smoking contributes to many health problems.

3. _____ Computers are used in offices, homes, and stores.

   _____ Computers are important in modern life.

4. _____ A visit to a petting zoo is a good activity for children.

   _____ Children can touch and hold the animals.

5. _____ Baseball card collectors learn a lot about the history of baseball.

   _____ Collecting baseball cards is entertaining as well as educational.

6. _____ George Washington Carver taught farmers how to rotate their crops.

   _____ Farmers owe a lot to George Washington Carver.

7. _____ My favorite place to visit in Mexico is Guadalajara.

   _____ There are many wonderful restaurants in Guadalajara, Mexico.

8. _____ One way to find out about a child-care center is to talk with parents.

   _____ How can you pick a good child-care center?

Topic Sentences, p. 2

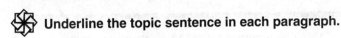 **Underline the topic sentence in each paragraph.**

9. He was, without question, the most adorable kitten Katya had ever seen. His dark green eyes were beautiful against his white coat, and he had four black paws. His large ears stood straight up, making his head look smaller than it really was. "I'm taking him home," she announced to the animal shelter volunteer.

10. The Arctic's climate is determined by the amount of heat and light received from the sun. Because of Earth's slant, Arctic regions don't get direct sunlight during certain parts of the year. The North Pole gets no direct sunlight for six consecutive months each year. In the summer, even though the Arctic gets long hours of sunlight, the slant of Earth doesn't allow as much heat to hit the region.

11. First, Jamal heard a beeping noise that sounded like his clothes dryer was off balance. Next, he saw the monitor flicker. The beeps turned into high-pitched whining noises. White lines shot across the screen and then the monitor turned completely black. Jamal's computer had just shut itself off for no apparent reason.

12. Its name means "king of the tyrant lizards." It stood up to 18 feet high and was between 40 and 50 feet long. It had two strong hind legs and two tiny arms. Tyrannosaurus Rex was the largest of all meat-eating dinosaurs. Some scientists think that it hunted live animals, but others think it lived on animals that had already been killed by other animals.

13. Mrs. Anaya's friends have an odd assortment of pets. Rosa has a boa constrictor that slithers freely around her house. Sara and Tony have a parrot that sings TV show theme songs. Mutan has a fish that swims sideways. Even Misha has a strange pet: a rabbit with one pink eye and one gray eye!

Name _____   Date _____

Supporting Details

- In a paragraph, all the sentences besides the topic sentence provide **supporting details** to explain or give information about the topic.
- Three kinds of supporting details are **reasons**, **examples**, and **facts**. A paragraph may use one, two, or all three kinds of details.

EXAMPLES:

reasons   My friend Sara would make a wonderful kindergarten teacher. She loves children and likes spending time with them. She always has a cheerful smile, a soft voice, and a kind word. Sara is clever at making up songs, games, and activities that young children enjoy. Perhaps most important is that she has enormous patience and rarely gets angry.

examples   Exercise has many benefits. It reduces stress and tension and helps a person develop a better psychological outlook. It also increases energy, improves sleeping habits, promotes better posture, and aids digestion. One of its most important benefits is protecting the body against injury and disease. Finally, exercise burns calories and helps a person maintain a desirable weight.

facts   Since World War II, Canada has developed from a largely rural economy to an affluent industrial society. Today it has more than 93,000 kilometers of rail lines and 880,000 kilometers of highways for moving raw materials and manufactured goods. The St. Lawrence Seaway and other waterways provide more than 3,000 additional kilometers for moving freight. Oil and natural gas are transported through 100,000 kilometers of pipelines. Modern ports handle imports and exports from all over the world.

 Choose a sentence that belongs with each topic sentence. Darken the circle by your answer.

1. Vegetables are my favorite food group.
   Ⓐ I like broccoli in all kinds of recipes.
   Ⓑ Meat is good, too.
   Ⓒ Sweets aren't good for you, but they are fun to eat.

2. The Grand Canyon is one of the most spectacular natural sights in North America.
   Ⓐ It is too crowded with tourists.
   Ⓑ It is about a mile deep, four to eighteen miles wide, and 217 miles long.
   Ⓒ I never want to visit the Grand Canyon.

3. Situation comedies, usually called sitcoms, are my favorite kind of TV show.
   Ⓐ I like TV movies, too.
   Ⓑ Sitcoms are short and entertaining.
   Ⓒ News programs provide important information.

4. If you want to travel outside the country, get a valid passport.
   Ⓐ Some places don't require a passport.
   Ⓑ You won't need a passport in Latin America.
   Ⓒ A valid passport is the best travel documentation available.

Supporting Details, p. 2

 Read the paragraphs. Underline the topic sentence in each.

5.   Some people think California is not a safe place to live. It has earthquakes that crumple buildings and flatten freeways. People never know when they'll wake up to find their houses shaking and furniture flying across the room. Wildfires frequently threaten homes, and people may lose everything they have. Traffic jams, riots, and air pollution also occur.

6.   Other people think California is the best place in the world to live. They love its mild climate and its casual lifestyle. They like the variety of having the beach, the mountains, and beautiful valleys close by. These people think California is exciting because so many different kinds of people and cultures can be found there. They think all the good things outweigh the bad ones.

Read each supporting detail. Write 1 if it belongs in Paragraph 1 above and 2 if it belongs in Paragraph 2.

_____   7. In 1994, more than 60 people died in the earthquake near Los Angeles.

_____   8. Venice Beach is a popular place for skating and people-watching.

_____   9. The Lake Tahoe area is a popular spot for skiing in the winter.

_____   10. The fertile valleys of California produce more fruits and vegetables than any other state.

_____   11. Some days the smog is so bad in Los Angeles that a dull brown haze hangs over the entire area.

_____   12. Long periods of drought sometimes cause rationing of water.

_____   13. San Francisco, Los Angeles, and San Diego are large cities with many cultural attractions.

Choose one of the following topic sentences. Then add two or three other sentences that tell more about the topic sentence.

a. I like movies that make me laugh.

b. There are many reasons why I like to listen to music.

c. Money isn't the answer to everyone's problems.

_____

_____

_____

_____

_____

_____

_____

Name _____   Date _____

Paragraph Unity

- Each sentence in a paragraph should support the topic sentence. This is called **paragraph unity**.
- Any sentence that doesn't help develop the topic sentence doesn't belong in the paragraph.

    EXAMPLE:

    Maple trees grow in the southern part of Quebec. They produce more maple syrup than trees in any other area in North America. <u>Everyone knows that maple syrup tastes really good</u>. Many Canadians enjoy attending the annual Maple Festival each March when the syrup is collected.

    This sentence doesn't support the topic sentence. It should be removed.

 Underline the sentence or sentences in each paragraph that do not belong.

1. The Chinese calendar, based on a twelve-year cycle, is the oldest continuously used calendar. Each year in the cycle is named for an animal: sheep, monkey, rooster, dog, pig, rat, ox, tiger, hare, dragon, snake, horse. It is said that the animal's characteristics belong to a person born that year as well as to the year itself. The Chinese don't usually celebrate their birthdays the same way that people in western cultures do.

2. Hu-lan walked down the peaceful country road. She listened to the soft breeze rustle through the leaves overhead and thought about how different it was from the noisy city streets of home. Hu-lan was named after her great-grandmother. Her father was an engineer. Hu-lan closed her eyes and felt the sun's warmth on her face. She knew it was wise to vacation in the country. "I'll go home truly relaxed," she thought to herself.

3. For very young children, play is the chief method of learning. Games like "peek-a-boo" teach babies that parents will come back even when they go away. Sometimes parents of young children talk with other parents who have children the same age as their own. Puzzles, blocks, and balls teach hand-eye coordination. They also help children use large and small muscles.

 Write a paragraph about your favorite book or TV show. Write a topic sentence and three or four other sentences that support the topic. Use your own paper.

Name _____   Date _____

Transition

> • Sentences in a paragraph should be connected so that thoughts flow smoothly.
> • **Transition words** and **transition phrases** show how one idea leads to another.
>
> EXAMPLES:
> **transition words:**
>
> | | | |
> |---|---|---|
> | after | also | another |
> | consequently | finally | first |
> | furthermore | however | last |
> | next | then | therefore |
>
> EXAMPLES:
> **transition phrases:**
>
> | | | |
> |---|---|---|
> | after that | at last | at the same time |
> | for example | in the meantime | on the other hand |

 Circle the transition word(s) or phrase(s) in each paragraph.

1.   Walking is good for the body and the brain. (For example,) walking helps the heart and lungs work more efficiently. It also helps reduce blood pressure. At the same time, it helps the body burn excess calories. Furthermore, people who walk regularly report less stress and a more positive outlook on life.

2.   Making a quilt requires skill and planning. First, you choose a pattern and create templates or pattern pieces. Then, you calculate the amount of fabric you need. Next, you cut out the fabric. After that, you sew each quilt piece together. After you complete the quilt top, you sew it to the bottom fabric with some padding in between. Finally, you quilt the piece.

 Write a transition word or phrase to show the connection between each set of sentences.

3. The secretary forgot her pencil and pad. _____ therefore _____ She couldn't take notes at today's meeting.

4. Washing a car is not an easy task. _____ Even when you spend lots of time scrubbing and polishing, you can miss spots.

5. Sarita's brother has a wonderful sense of humor. _____ Sometimes he is in a grumpy mood.

6. Mix the cake batter. _____ Pour it in a pan.

7. Harrison ordered decorations for the dance, but he didn't know the size of the hall.

_____ Half the hall had to be left undecorated.

Logical Order

- Sentences in a paragraph should be arranged in an order that makes sense. This is called **logical order**.
- One kind of logical order is **time order**.
  EXAMPLES:

  Orlando swam though the coral reef, feeling the gentle tug of the current on his hair. An eel slithered in front of him and disappeared into the reef behind a rock. After collecting a few samples, Orlando looked at the pressure gauge attached to his scuba tank. He noticed the air level was getting low, so he decided to end his dive. He slowly began to swim back up to the waiting boat.

  When you work in a laboratory, you may want to follow a few simple safety procedures. First, make sure that all chemicals are labeled properly. Second, make sure there are fire extinguishers and first-aid kits within reach. Finally, have proper eye protection, such as goggles, to wear when conducting or observing experiments.

 Number each set of sentences in logical order. Then write the reordered paragraph on your own paper.

1. _____ They followed the suggestions in a book about home gardening.

   _____ Mrs. Gordino laid out the rows and planted the seeds they had bought, covering them carefully.

   __1__ Mr. and Mrs. Gordino had spent many days in the backyard preparing the ground for planting.

   _____ They continued to sprinkle the garden plot daily, until one sunny morning, two purple flowers appeared.

   _____ Mrs. Gordino added fertilizer and pulled weeds.

2. _____ Another option is to call a local animal shelter or hospital to get a recommendation from the experts in those places.

   _____ If you own a pet, it is important to choose a veterinarian before you need one.

   _____ You may want to ask a friend or family member to recommend one.

   _____ Make sure that you and your pet feel comfortable with the veterinarian.

3. _____ People can change their diet and exercise habits so that they minimize the risks.

   _____ Can you avoid heart disease?

   _____ By selecting healthier foods, cutting out excess fat, and stopping smoking, people can significantly lower their risk of heart disease.

   _____ High blood cholesterol, cigarette smoking, and high blood pressure are the three major risk factors for heart disease.

Name _____   Date _____

Clarity

- Good writing has **clarity**, or clear meaning. Sometimes writing is unclear because not enough information is given.
  - EXAMPLES:
    - Did Anton tell Margarita as much as Meg?   (unclear)
    - Did Anton tell Margarita as much as he told Meg?   (clear)
- Sometimes sentences are unclear because important words that connect ideas have been left out.
  - EXAMPLES:
    - A strange, cold draft began to chill us, a scary adventure.   (unclear)
    - A strange, cold draft began to chill us. Being lost in the cave was becoming a scary adventure.   (clear)

 Underline the unclear word or words in each sentence. Then rewrite each sentence to make it clear. You may want to add words or change words.

1. I gave you more ice cream than <u>he</u>.

    I gave you more ice cream than he did.

2. Yoshi was selling dolls at the crafts fair, a group of handmade ones.

    _____

3. Benito has known Gina longer than Marie.

    _____

4. On Halloween, Ms. Flores made a haunted house in her garage, frightening for some little children.

    _____

    _____

5. You can find many titles of books about stamp collecting in the library, but only with a current library card.

    _____

    _____

    _____

6. Brad's toolbox has some valuable tools, given to him by his father.

    _____

    _____

    _____

7. His hat was floppy, getting in his eyes was a problem.

    _____

    _____

Name _____   Date _____

Concise Sentences

- Sentences are **concise** when they contain only the words they need.
- To get rid of **wordiness**, leave out unnecessary words and phrases or substitute simple, clear words for them.

  EXAMPLES:
  Just as he got the fish off the hook, it slipped and fell back into the water. (wordy)
  As he unhooked the fish, it slipped and fell into the water.   (concise)
  His model airplane, it broke its wing.   (wordy)
  The wing on his model airplane broke.   (concise)
  His model airplane had a broken wing.   (concise)
  Not very long after that happened, Eli knew he had won.   (wordy)
  Soon after that, Eli knew he had won.   (concise)

 Rewrite each sentence to make it more concise.

1. Lidia couldn't come with us on account of she had to go to work.

   _____Lidia couldn't come with us because she had to work._____

2. Ruben went to the grocery store, but before he went, he made a list of all the many things he wanted to buy.

   _____

   _____

3. The students who are in their first year of college are buying books at the bookstore.

   _____

   _____

4. This time of the year, with all its many colors, it is my most favorite.

   _____

   _____

5. Dee knew she was going to pass the test because of the fact that she had studied really hard for many days and nights before the test.

   _____

   _____

   _____

Concise Sentences, p. 2

- **Combining sentences** is another way to eliminate wordiness and make writing more concise.
  EXAMPLES:
     Mr. Nguyen told us about his next-door neighbor. Mr. Nguyen's next-door neighbor's name is Randy Park, and he appeared on a television talk show.   (wordy)
     Mr. Nguyen's next-door neighbor, Randy Park, appeared on a television talk show.   (concise, combined into one sentence)

 Combine each set of sentences into one sentence to eliminate wordiness.

6. Clara's grandfather was a very tall man. Her grandfather had a large mole on his forehead. He had dark eyes, too.

   Clara's grandfather, a very tall man with dark eyes, had a large mole on his forehead.

7. Luis wrote the problem on the chalkboard for the class to see. His work still was not clear enough for the class to understand.

   _____

   _____

8. Dogs know how to bark. They also know how to protect their owners.

   _____

   _____

   _____

9. Three people won the contest. The reward was divided equally among the three contest winners.

   _____

   _____

   _____

10. Marta went to the basketball game. She was expecting to meet some friends. She had invited her friends, and she told them to meet her at the ticket booth.

   _____

   _____

11. The old two-story house is losing its shingles. The house was built over a hundred years ago.

   _____

   _____

 Write a short paragraph on your own paper about an interest or hobby you have. Then read over the paragraph and get rid of unnecessary words or phrases.

Name _____   Date _____

Unit 5 Test

Read the paragraphs below carefully. Decide how the sentences in each paragraph can be improved. Use the paragraphs to answer the questions. Darken the circle by your answer.

(1) Can you imagine what life would be like without clocks? (2) The only way to tell what time it was would be to look at the light from the sun. (3) When the sun rose, it would be daytime. (4) No one would know the exact time of day. (5) Everyone would do things at different times. (6) People wouldn't wake up on time. (7) People wouldn't get to work on time.

(8) But by measuring sunlight and shadow, people marked time on the first clocks. (9) The first devices for measuring time were probably shadow sticks by the early Egyptians. (10) They cast shadows as the sun moved across the sky. (11) The Egyptians also built the pyramids. (12) Perhaps the best known type of shadow clock is the sundial. (13) The Romans added numbers to the sundial. (14) The numbers represented the hours in a day. (15) There is one big problem with sundials. (16) It is that they only work when the sun is shining.

(17) Later clocks solved that problem. (18) Water clocks used water flowing from one container to another at a steady rate. (19) Hourglasses used sand flowing from one container to another at a steady rate. (20) The water or sand drained away. (21) It was measured. (22) The measurement told how much time had passed. (23) Pendulum clocks and mechanical watches used a coiled spring to measure time. (24) It unwound a little bit at a time. (25) I like digital watches. (26) In the twentieth century, electric and atomic clocks were developed as the most accurate ways to measure time so far.

1. How should sentence 2 be written to make it concise?

Ⓐ The only way to tell for sure what time it is is to look at the sun.

Ⓑ The only way to tell time would be by sunlight.

Ⓒ Leave it as it is.

2. What transition word or phrase could be added to the beginning of sentence 4?

Ⓐ Furthermore   Ⓑ However   Ⓒ In the meantime

3. What transition word or phrase could be added to the beginning of sentence 5?

Ⓐ Consequently   Ⓑ At last   Ⓒ Next

4. What transition word or phrase could be added to the beginning of sentence 6?

Ⓐ Another   Ⓑ Last   Ⓒ For example

5. What transition word or phrase could be added to the beginning of sentence 7?

Ⓐ In addition   Ⓑ Last   Ⓒ First

6. Which sentence is the topic sentence of the second paragraph?

Ⓐ sentence 8   Ⓑ sentence 10   Ⓒ sentence 14

Unit 5 Test, p. 2

7. How should sentence 9 be rewritten to make it clear?

   Ⓐ Add the word <u>maybe</u> at the beginning of the sentence.

   Ⓑ Add the word <u>used</u> after the word <u>sticks</u>.

   Ⓒ Remove the word <u>Egyptians</u>.

8. Sentence 11 should _____.

   Ⓐ remain as it is   Ⓑ be left out   Ⓒ move before sentence 10

9. Sentence 14 should _____.

   Ⓐ be combined with sentence 12

   Ⓑ be combined with sentence 13

   Ⓒ be left out

10. Sentence 16 should _____.

   Ⓐ move before sentence 13

   Ⓑ omit the words <u>is shining</u>

   Ⓒ combine with sentence 15

11. Which sentence is the topic sentence of the third paragraph?

   Ⓐ sentence 17   Ⓑ sentence 19   Ⓒ sentence 26

12. Sentences 18 and 19 should _____.

   Ⓐ move after sentence 22

   Ⓑ be left out

   Ⓒ be combined

13. Sentence 21 should _____.

   Ⓐ be left out

   Ⓑ combine with sentence 20

   Ⓒ move after sentence 22

14. Which is the best way to combine sentences 23 and 24?

   Ⓐ To measure time, pendulum clocks and mechanical watches used a coiled spring that slowly unwound.

   Ⓑ Clocks and watches used springs.

   Ⓒ Pendulum clocks measured time, and mechanical watches used a coiled spring.

15. Sentence 25 should _____.

   Ⓐ be left as it is

   Ⓑ move to become the last sentence

   Ⓒ be left out

16. What transition word or phrase could be added to the beginning of sentence 26?

   Ⓐ On the other hand   Ⓑ However   Ⓒ Finally

Answer Key

Assessment
Pages 7–10
1. S
2. H
3. A
4. S
5. wind
6. S
7. C
8. P
9. P
10. C
11. S
12. she would
13. must not
14. a

The words in bold should be circled.

15. E; foot; **is**
16. IM; (You); **place**
17. IN; you; **did forget**
18. D; members; **will meet**
19. CS
20. CP
21. RO
22. CS
23. I
24. common nouns: trip; proper nouns: Miss Matson, Jennifer, Los Angeles
25. past
26. future
27. present
28. future
29. is; are
30. will drive
31. teach
32. Set; sitting

The words in bold should be circled.

33. IP, **Somebody**
34. OP, **me**
35. PP, **its**
36. SP, **I**
37. his, **Gilberto**
38. their, **Bill and Ariana**
39. adjective
40. adverb
41. adjective
42. adjective
43. adjective
44. adverb

The words in bold should be circled.

45. in the largest room; of the hotel; and; in attendance
46. on the corner; or; off the market
47. A
48. B
49. A
50. D
51. B
52. D
53. B
54. C
55. B
56. B
57. B
58. C
59. B
60. C
61. C
62. I
63. C
64. I
65. I
66. C
67. C
68. I
69. C
70. B
71. Students should circle the first sentence and underline all other sentences except "Edison also invented electricity."
72. 3
73. 1
74. 2
75. 4

Unit 1
Page 11
Answers will vary.

Page 12
1. ring, wring
2. sail, sale
3. browse
4. days, inn
5. son
6. boulder
7. pier, peer, sea
8. loan
9. mist
10. red, blue, rain
11. threw, through
12. buy, by
13. hour, our, aisle
14. principal
15. meets, Capitol
16. led, horse, reins
17. brakes
18. There
19. straight
20. allowed
21. tow
22. shown
23. way, weigh
24. to, two, too
25. pane
26. knew, new
27. their
28. ate, eight
29. sea, see
30. bored, board

Page 13
1. b
2. b
3. a
4. b
5. b
6. a
7. b
8. b
9. a
10. a
11. fine
12. snap
13. well
14. fair
15. lock

Page 14
Definitions may vary.
Possible responses:
1. impractical, not practical
2. misbehave, not behave
3. uneasy, not easy
4. nonviolent, not violent
5. unusual, not usual
6. un, not expected
7. dis, not appear
8. dis, not agree
9. mis, spell wrong
10. pre, view before
11. re, enter again
12. mis, place wrongly
13. im, not possible
14. non, not stop
15. un, not important
16. in, not sane
17. pre, judge before

Page 15
Definitions may vary.
Possible responses:
1. mountainous, full of mountains
2. comfortable, able to have comfort
3. snowy, pertaining to snow
4. teacher, person having to do with teaching
5. knowledgeable, able to have knowledge
6. able, able to be broken
7. less, without end
8. ous, full of hazard
9. able, able to be regretted
10. ous, full of poison
11. able, able to be depended upon
12. ous, full of humor
13. ful, full of tears
14. y, pertaining to bumps
15. less, without care
16. al, pertaining to nature
17. y, pertaining to dirt

Page 16
1. didn't
2. you'll
3. we're
4. isn't
5. who's
6. hadn't
7. I'll
8. we've
9. it's
10. don't
11. they've
12. wouldn't
13. won't
14. you'd
15. weren't
16. there's
17. couldn't
18. I've
19. she'll
20. they're
21. We're, We are
22. We'll, We will
23. it's, it is
24. He's, He is
25. he'll, he will
26. she's, she is
27. She'd, She would
28. would've, would have
29. weren't, were not
30. I've, I have

Page 17
1.–12. Answers will vary.
13.–17. Definitions may vary slightly.
13. a person who keeps the financial accounts
14. a boat that transports across a body of water
15. a person who has great authority over land
16. a booth where one pays a toll
17. a chair that moves back and forth

Pages 18–19
1. j
2. i
3. h
4. a
5. e
6. f
7. d
8. g
9. b
10. c

Meanings may vary.
11. see eye to eye, agree completely
12. keep their nose to the grindstone, work hard and steadily
13. gets his goat, annoys, irritates, or angers him
14. turn over a new leaf, make a new start
15. stick to his guns, be firm, not retreat from his plan
16. blew his top, lost his temper, got mad
17. beat around the bush, talk about something without getting to the point
18. hit the books, study hard
19. kick up his heels, have a good time, be lively or merry
20. spilled the beans, let the secret out, told someone
21. in hot water, in trouble
22. to eat crow, admit to being wrong
23. just water under the bridge, something over, past, or too late to do anything about
24. a
25. e
26. b
27. c
28. d
29. f
30. Answers will vary.

Unit 1 Test
Pages 20–21
1. A
2. S
3. H
4. HG
5. S
6. A
7. HG
8. H
9. S
10. H
11. H
12. A
13. S
14. HG
15. A
16. im, not possible
17. y, like or pertaining to rust
18. ous, full of hazard
19. in, not complete
20. un, not easy
21. non, not violent
22. less, without help
23. ful, full of beauty
24. Where is, air/plane

120

Answer Key
Language: Usage and Practice HS, SV 1419027867

25. it is, down/town
26. Is not, head/quarters
27. they are, high/rise
28. can not, roof/top
29. hang in there, stay with something, persevere
30. get in touch with, speak with or see someone

31. C	38. B
32. C	39. C
33. B	40. C
34. C	41. C
35. A	42. A
36. B	43. B
37. B	44. C

Unit 2
Pages 22–23
Items 1, 3, 5, 7, 10, 13, 14, 16, 21, 22, 24, 27, 28, 30, 33, 35, 37, 38, 39, 40, 41, 44, 47, 48, 49, 50, 52, 56, 57, 60 are sentences. Each sentence should end with a period.
61.–62. Rewritten fragments will vary.

Pages 24–25
1. IN (?)	28. E (!)
2. IN (?)	29. IM (.)
3. IM (.)	30. D (.)
4. D (.)	31. IN (?)
5. E (!)	32. IM (.)
6. IN (?)	33. IM (.)
7. IM (.)	34. D (.)
8. D (.)	35. D (.)
9. E (!) or IM (.)	36. IN (?)
10. IM (.)	37. E (!)
11. D (.)	38. IN (?)
12. D (.) or E (!)	39. D (.)
13. IN (?)	40. D (.)
14. IN (?)	41. IM (.)
15. IM (.)	42. D (.)
16. D (.)	43. IM (.)
17. IM (.) or E (!)	44. IN (?)
18. D (.)	45. IM (.)
19. IN (?)	46. IN (?)
20. D (.)	47. IN (?)
21. IM (.)	48. D (.)
22. IN (?)	49. IN (?)
23. D (.)	50. IM (.)
24. E (!) or IM (.)	51. E (!) or IM (.)
25. IM (.)	
26. D (.)	52. IM (.)
27. IM (.)	53. IN (?)

Sentences will vary.

Pages 26–27
1. (?)	7. (.)
2. (.)	8. (.)
3. (?)	9. (?)
4. (.)	10. (?)
5. (.)	11. (?)
6. (?)	12. (.)

13. (.)	37. (!)
14. (?)	38. (.)
15. (?)	39. (!)
16. (.)	40. (!)
17. (?)	41. (!)
18. (?)	42. (!)
19. (.)	43. (!), (.) or (!)
20. (.)	
21. (?)	44. (.)
22. (?)	45. (!) or (.)
23. (.)	46. (.)
24. (.)	47. (.)
25. (?)	48. (!), (!)
26. (.)	49. (.)
27. (?)	50. (.)
28. (?)	51. (!), (!)
29. (?)	52. (!)
30. (.)	53. (!) or (.)
31. (!)	54. (!), (!), (!)
32. (!), (!)	55. (.)
33. (.)	56. (.)
34. (.)	57. (!)
35. (!), (!)	58. (!)
36. (.)	59. (.)

Pages 28–29
1. Amy / built
2. cleaner / will remove
3. waltzes / were composed
4. Queen Victoria / ruled
5. people / are waiting
6. visit / was
7. rocket / was
8. meeting / was held
9. farmers / are harvesting
10. house / has
11. heart / pumps
12. computer / will help
13. friend / has moved
14. silence / fell
15. officers / were stopping
16. chef / prepared
17. father / is
18. José Salazar / is running
19. Lightning / struck
20. Magazines about bicycling / are becoming
21. They / answered
22. twilight / came
23. Willy / has
24. country / has
25. We / will have
26. truck / was
27.–52. Sentences will vary.

Pages 30–31
Words in bold print should be underlined twice.
1. The different meanings for that word / **cover**
2. A valuable oil / **is made**
3. A beautiful highway / **winds**
4. The lady in the black dress / **studied**
5. The meadowlark / **builds**
6. A rare Chinese vase / **was**
7. Many stories / **have been written**
8. His answer to the question / **was**
9. Every sentence / **should begin**
10. All of the group / **went**
11. In Norway, a narrow inlet of the sea between cliffs / **is called**
12. The Dutch / **grew**
13. The two U.S. treasury mints / **are located**
14. Benjamin Franklin's *Poor Richard's Almanac* / **is filled**
15. The warm climate of Florida / **attracts**
16. That movie / **has been shown**
17. Acres of wheat / **rippled**
18. That mechanic / **completed**
19. The people in that picture / **were boarding**
20. One / **can find**
21. The city of Albuquerque / **is**
22. The apple trees / **have**
23. Sequoias, the world's tallest trees, / **are found**
24. John Banister / **was**
25. The tall pine trees / **hide**
26. The lady / **filled**
27. A sudden clap of thunder / **frightened**
28. The soft snow / **covered**
29. We / **drove**
30. Suzanne's friend / **got**
31. Our class / **read**
32. Maria's little boys / **were playing**
33. This album / **has**
34. We / **are making**
35. All of the trees on that lawn / **are**
36. Many Americans / **are working**
37. The manager / **read**
38. Jerome / **brought**
39. We / **opened**
40. The two mechanics / **worked**
41. Black and yellow butterflies / **fluttered**
42. The little girl / **spoke**
43. We / **found**
44. The best part of the program / **is**
45. Every ambitious person / **is working**
46. Sheryl / **swam**
47. Our program / **will begin**
48. The handle of this basket / **is**
49. The clock in the tower / **strikes**
50. The white farmhouse on that road / **belongs**
51. The first game of the season / **will be played**
52. The plants / **sprouted**
53. The television program / **was**
54. I / **used**
55. My brother's truck / **is**
56.–57. Sentences will vary.

Page 32
1. CS; Arturo and I / often work late on Friday.
2. SS; Sandy / left the person near the crowded exit.
3. CS; She and I / will mail the packages to San Francisco today.
4. CS; Detroit and Chicago / are two frequently visited cities.
5. SS; The fire / spread rapidly to other buildings in the neighborhood.
6. CS; Luis and Tara / helped their children with their homework.
7. CS; Swimming, jogging, and hiking / were our favorite sports.
8. CS; Melbourne and Sydney / are important Australian cities.
9. CS; Eric and I / had an interesting experience Saturday.
10. CS; The Red Sea and the Mediterranean Sea / are connected by the Suez Canal.
11. CS; The Astros and the Angels / are two baseball teams.
12. SS; The people / waved to us from the top of the cliff.
13. CS; Hiroshi and Ron / helped us move to our new apartment.

Language: Usage and Practice HS, SV 1419027867

14. CS; Clean clothes and a neat appearance / are important in an interview.
15. CS; Raymond's son and his faithful dog / are never far apart.
16. CS; Dave and Pablo / are on their way to the swimming pool.
17. SS; Thomas / combed his daughter's shiny black hair.
18. CS; Redbud and dogwood trees / bloom in the spring.
19. SS; I / hummed a cheerful tune on the way to the meeting.
20. CS; Buffalo, deer, and antelope / roamed the plains.
21. CS; Livia and her sister / are very talented singers.
22. CS; Vancouver and Calgary / are two cities in Canada.
23. SS; Hang gliding / is a popular sport in Hawaii.
24. SS; Our neighbors / asked us to come for dinner on Tuesday.
25. SS; The doctor / asked him to get a blood test.
26.–27. Sentences will vary.

Page 33
1. CP; Jarrell / grinned and nodded.
2. SP; Plants / need air to live.
3. SP; Old silver tea kettles / were among their possessions.
4. CP; My aunt / buys and sells real estate.
5. SP; Snow / covered every highway in the county.
6. CP; Mr. Sander / designs and makes odd pieces of furniture.
7. SP; Popcorn / is one of my favorite snack foods.
8. SP; Aerobic dancing / is a good way to stay fit.
9. CP; The ducks / crossed the road and found the ducklings.
10. CP; They / came early and stayed late.
11. SP; Crystal / participated in the Special Olympics this year.

12. CP; Marci / raked and sacked the leaves.
13. CP; Perry / built the fire and cooked supper.
14. SP; We / collected old newspapers for the recycling center.
15. SP; Daniel / arrived in Cincinnati during the afternoon.
16. SP; Jenny's parents / are visiting in Oregon and Washington.
17. SP; The Garzas / live in that apartment building on Oak Street.
18. CP; Alex and his crew / picked up and delivered the shingles today.
19. CP; The audience / talked and laughed before the performance.
20. CP; Automobiles / crowd and jam that highway early in the morning.
21. SP; The apples / are rotting in the boxes.
22. CP; The leader of the group / grumbled and scolded.
23. CP; She / worked hard and waited patiently.
24. SP; Benjamin Franklin / was a great American.
25. SP; The supervisor / has completed the work for the week.
26.–27. Sentences will vary.

Page 34
Words in bold print should be underlined twice.
1. The movie **is playing** when?
2. I **will** never **forget** my first train trip.
3. The best picture in the poster shop **is** here.
4. He **has** seldom **been** ill.
5. The lights **went** out.
6. Bookcases **were** there on all sides of the room.
7. The speeding car **swerved** around the sharp curve.
8. (You) **get** out of the swimming pool during the rainstorm.
9. Two children **are** still there in the pool.

Page 35
1. S; world / are
2. C; Earth / is ... it / is

3. S; world / are
4. C; We / cannot ... we / cannot
5. S; water / comes
6. S; water / is
7. The Pacific Ocean is the world's largest ocean, and it covers more area than all the land put together.
8. Smaller bodies of salt water are called seas, gulfs, or bays, and they are often encircled by land.
9. Seas, gulfs, and bays are joined to the oceans, and they vary in size and depth.
10. You could spend your vacation at the Mediterranean, or you could spend your vacation touring Asia.

Pages 36–37
1. R
2. C
3. R
4. R
5. C
6. R
7. R
8. C
9. C
10. C
11. C
12. R
13. C
14. R
15. R
16.–21. Answers will vary.

Unit 2 Test
Pages 38–39
1. D (.)
2. D (.)
3. IM (.)
4. F
5. D (.)
6. D (.) or E (!)
7. IN (?)
8. F
9. E (!)
Rewritten sentences will vary. Possible responses:
10. Justin needed to buy a gallon of milk.
11. He could not buy any because the store was closed when he got there.
12. Then he drove around lost for over an hour.
13. The problem was he did not know where he was going.
Words in bold print should be underlined twice.
14. You / **must guess** the number of beans in the jar.
15. Jon / **will write** his guesses on these pieces of paper.
16. On the counter **can be found** / pencils.

17. Melinda / **has** already **written** her guess.
18. They / **are** eager to find the answer.
19. Jon / **is** the winner.
20. Pencils can be found on the counter.
21. CP
22. CS
23. C
24. CP
25. CS
26. CP
27. C
28. C
29. CS
Students should write RO before 31, 33, 34.
Rewritten sentences may vary. Possible responses:
36. Games have been around for thousands of years. In Egypt alone at least four games were played as early as 2700 B.C.
37. New games are being created all the time; only some will stand the test of time.
38. I have an idea for a new game. Would you like to play it?

Unit 3
Page 40
1. Lupe Garza, years, supervisor
2. piece, land, triangle, mouth, river, delta
3. Gilbert Stuart, portraits, presidents, United States
4. Albert Einstein, scientists, history, Germany
5. library, world, Alexandria, Egypt
6. Jim Thorpe, Sac Indian, athletes, world
7. Mahalia Jackson, singer, songs, spirituals
8. Marconi, telegraph
9. parades, football, television, New Year's Day
10. Pocahontas, daughter, Powhatan, life, Captain John Smith
11. *Boston News-Letter*, newspaper, United States
12. message, English Channel, century
13. Chicago, city, Lake Michigan
14. house, street, trees
15. Mei, job, Shoppers World

16. Nova Scotia, Prince Edward Island
17. Washington, D.C., capital, United States
18. Potatoes, apples, crops, provinces, Canada
19. Jessica, car
20. Hailstones, raindrops, snowflakes
21. days, summer
22. rivers, North America, explorers
23. Trey, bookshelves, apartment
24. California, home, stars, movies
25. William Caxton, book, England
26. Christi, tomatoes, lettuce, cherries, market
27. building, offices, stores, apartments
28. Marcy, Peoria, daughter
29. airport, hours, snowstorm
30. pen, ink

Page 41
1. timber, oak, furniture, bridges, ships
2. painter, jeweler, farmer, engineer, inventor
3. crops, sugar, tobacco, coffee, fruits
4. groves, pecans, part
5. rivers, waterfalls, lakes
6. bridge, kind, world
7. foods, lamb, fish, olives, cheese
8. road, tunnel, base, tree
9. civilizations, gold, ornaments
10. lakes
11. tree, blossoms, fruit, orange
12. center, entertainment
13. United States
14. William Penn, Pennsylvania
15. Elm Grove Library, Amy Tan
16. Commander Byrd, North Pole
17. Dr. Jeanne Spurlock, Howard University College of Medicine
18. Europe, Asia
19. Colombia
20. Mount Kilimanjaro, Africa
21. Navajo Indians
22. Leticia, Carlos, Samantha, Ted
23. Thomas Jefferson, United States

24. Lake Michigan
25. Quebec, North America

Pages 42–43
1. counties
2. waltzes
3. tomatoes
4. mice
5. matches
6. calves
7. centuries
8. trenches
9. bookcases
10. pianos
11. desks
12. geese
13. radios
14. flies
15. children
16. dresses
17. brushes
18. lunches
19. countries
20. benches
21. earrings
22. counties
23. pianos
24. foxes
25. checkers
26. potatoes
27. dishes
28. stores
29. pennies
30. dresses
31. bridges
32. cities
33. deer
34. flashes
35. coaches
36. e's
37. mice
38. boxes
39. scarves
40. n's
41. radios
42. 90's
43. women

Pages 44–45
1. Steve's
2. mother's
3. sister's
4. speaker's
5. collectors'
6. Rosie's, child's
7. Tarrens'
8. president's
9. mayor's
10. Anthony's
11. women's
12. family's
13. day's
14. lifeguard's
15. store's
16. children's
17. Harry's
18. Jim's
19. Darrell's
20. Lees'
21. Mark's
22. Frank's, Alex's
23. neighbors'
24. Kashons'
25. Canada's
26. girl's
27. child's
28. women's
29. children's
30. Jason's
31. Julia's
32. students'
33. father's
34. babies'
35. dog's
36. baby's
37. boys'
38. teacher's
39. Dr. Kay's
40. ladies'
41. table's
42. mothers'
43. players'
44. nieces'
45. club's
46. brother's
47. soldier's
48. men's
49. aunt's
50. writers'
51. waiter's
52. driver's
53. bird's
54. actors'
55. cats'
56. Rick's cap
57. Katy's wrench
58. the baby's cry
59. my cousins' house
60. Kim's new shoes
61. the dog's collar
62. Enrique's books
63. the superintendent's office
64. our neighbors' friends
65. the editor's opinion
66. the children's lunches
67. Mei Ling's coat
68. the teacher's assignment
69. the boy's babysitter
70. the manager's keys

Page 46
1. fewer
2. this
3. little
4. few
5. a number of
6. many
7. a little
8. much
9. less
10. a lot of
11. a few
12. that
13. a number of
14. a great deal of
15. several
16. a lot of
17. a few
18. fewer
19. little

Page 47
1. are
2. wrote
3. Check
4. have
5. is
6. reached
7. won
8. trains
9. wears
10. are
11. remember
12. bought
13. is
14. followed
15. whistled
16. watches
17. scored
18. won
19. is
20. is
21. set
22. Answer
23. explained
24. worked
25. has
26. plays
27. Brush
28. whirled
29. arrived
30. is

Page 48
1. Watch
2. dusted
3. copy
4. burned
5. fell
6. play
7. practiced
8. dashed
9. expresses
10. enjoys
11. leads
12. snowed
13. hiked
14. made
15. hand
16. Draw
17. skated
18. answered
19. repaired
20. suffered
21. Address
22. moved
23. worked
24. directs
25. played
26. walked
27. helped
28. collapsed
29. ticked
30. ate
31. cheered

Page 49
1. appears
2. is
3. was
4. is
5. looks
6. are
7. smell
8. feels
9. sounds
10. seems

11. is
12. feels
13. is
14. was
15. is
Answers may vary.
16. looks
17. are
18. seems
19. tastes
20. are
21. was
22. was
23. seemed
24. became
25. appeared
26. is
27. am
28. is
29. are
30. is

Page 50
1. were held
2. invented
3. was
4. was
5. built
6. will arrive
7. was
8. has made
9. covered
10. have ridden
11. is molding
12. spent
13. posted
14. has found
15. is going
16. have trimmed
17. exports
18. is reading
19. helped
20. was discovered
21. was called
22. are planning
23. has howled
24. have arrived
25. have written
26. can name
27. received
28. was
29. are working
30. had painted

Pages 51–52
Words in bold print should be circled.
1. **have** begun
2. **will** rake
3. **must** clean
4. **will** wash
5. **might** prepare
6. **should** wash
7. **would** make
8. **is** working
9. **has** sprayed
10. **must** close
11. **would** enjoy
12. **might** finish
13. **must** arrive
14. **Did** like
15. **may** paint
16. **is** visiting
17. **had** practiced
18. **will** drive
19. **has** read
20. **were** playing
21. **had** begun
22. **will** drive
23. **will** eat
24. **Do** want
25. **shall** enter
26. **will be** given

Answer Key
Language: Usage and Practice HS, SV 1419027867

27. **have been** studying
28. **may be** forming
29. **should be** reviewing
30. **Are** joining
31. **May** meet
32. **should have** known
33. **have** been
34. **have been** looking
35. **would have** met
36. **has been** delayed
37. **Would** prefer
38. **had been** enjoying
39. **has been** waiting
40. **had** been
41. **Will be** swimming
42. **must have been** splashing
43. **Can** take
44. **have** signed
45. **have been** practicing
46. **Will** tell
47. **Has** seen
48. **had been** wanting
49. **will** be
50. **will** buy
51. **has been** hitting
52. **has** eaten

Page 53
1. stories (P), tell
2. story (S), says
3. Wild Dog (S), becomes
4. dogs (P), leave
5. dog (S), doesn't
6. people (P), haven't
7. Studies (P), prove
8. Bones (P), have
9. vases (P), picture
10. organization (S), trains
11. eyes (P), have
12. dog (S), does
13. society (S), doesn't
14. Dogs (P), are
15. dog (S), needs
16. Dogs (P), find
17. people (P), agree
18. dog (S), doesn't
19. Dogs (P), like

Pages 54–55
1. future
2. past
3. past
4. present
5. future
6. present
7. past
8. future
9. past
10. present
11. Carmen's little dog followed her everywhere.
12. He barked and jumped at her heels.
13. He walked along behind her, and he even traveled in the car with her.
14. will arrive

15. will pick
16. walked
17. needed
18. watches
19. will walk
20. seems
21. visited
22. washed
23. dances
24. will train
25. prepared
26. started
27. will inform
28. live, present
29. take, present
30. play, present
31. threw, past
32. sailed, past
33. ran, past
34. shouted, past
35. listens, present
36. got, past
37. called, past
38. will play, future

Page 56
1. (is) stopping; stopped; (has) stopped
2. (is) listening; listened; (has) listened
3. (is) carrying; carried; (has) carried
4. (is) helping; helped; (has) helped
5. (is) starting; started; (has) started
6. (is) borrowing; borrowed; (has) borrowed
7. (is) calling; called; (has) called
8. (is) receiving; received; (has) received
9. (is) hoping; hoped; (has) hoped
10. (is) illustrating; illustrated; (has) illustrated
11. (is) dividing; divided; (has) divided
12. (is) changing; changed; (has) changed
13. (is) living; lived; (has) lived
14. (is) ironing; ironed; (has) ironed
15. (is) collecting; collected; (has) collected

Pages 57–58
1. (is) coming; came; (has) come
2. (is) eating; ate; (has) eaten
3. (is) seeing; saw; (has) seen
4. (is) taking; took; (has) taken
5. saw
6. taking
7. seeing
8. taken
9. eaten
10. took
11. did
12. done
13. come
14. ate
15. seen
16. came

17. (is) beginning; began; (has) begun
18. (is) going; went; (has) gone
19. (is) driving; drove; (has) driven
20. (is) giving; gave; (has) given
21. (is) running; ran; (has) run
22. gave
23. ran
24. gone
25. began
26. driving
27. driven
28. given
29. beginning
30. run
31. went
32. began
33. given
34. going
35. ran
36. given
37. gave
38. begun
39. drove
40. began
41. running

Pages 59–60
1. (is) growing; grew; (has) grown
2. (is) knowing; knew; (has) known
3. (is) ringing; rang; (has) rung
4. (is) singing; sang; (has) sung
5. (is) speaking; spoke; (has) spoken
6. sung
7. grew
8. knew
9. grown
10. singing
11. rung
12. grown
13. spoke
14. rang
15. spoken
16. speaking
17. sang
18. known
19. rang
20. spoken
21. grown
22. known
23. growing
24. rang
25. spoken
26. (is) blowing; blew; (has) blown
27. (is) breaking; broke; (has) broken
28. (is) choosing; chose; (has) chosen
29. (is) drawing; drew; (has) drawn
30. (is) flying; flew; (has) flown
31. drawn
32. blew
33. flying
34. chose
35. chosen
36. blown
37. broke
38. broken
39. choosing
40. drew
41. broken
42. broke
43. chosen
44. flown
45. broke
46. chosen
47. broke
48. drawn
49. breaking
50. drawn

Page 61
1. took
2. had
3. was
4. will take
5. will pick
6. bought
7. hopes
8. shops (buys) or (shopped) bought
9. looks (doesn't) or (looked) didn't
10. gets (starts) or (got) started
11. (comes) sit or came (sat)
12. (clean) finish or cleaned (had finished)
13. turns (watches) or (turned) watched
14. falls (sits) or (fell) sat

Page 62
1. is
2. is
3. is
4. is
5. are
6. is
7. are
8. Are
9. is
10. is
11. were, was
12. Were
13. was
14. were
15. were
16. weren't
17. weren't
18. were
19. weren't
20. was
21. was
22. was
23. was
24. Were
25. were
26. Weren't

Page 63
1. There are
2. There was
3. There were
4. There were
5. There are
6. There were
7. There were
8. There were
9. there are
10. There are
11. There are
12. There are
13. There is
14. There are
15. There are
16. There is
17. There are
18. There are
19. There were
20. There are
21. There is
22. There were
23. There was
24. There were
25. There were
26. There were
27. There are
28. there were
29. There are

Page 64
1. doesn't
2. did
3. done
4. doesn't
5. did
6. Don't
7. done
8. Don't
9. doesn't
10. don't
11. done
12. did
13. Doesn't
14. Doesn't
15. done
16. doesn't
17. don't
18. doesn't
19. don't
20. did
21. don't
22. done
23. doesn't
24. Don't

Page 65

1. lies
2. Lay
3. lying
4. lie
5. laid
6. laid
7. lie
8. lie
9. laid
10. lie
11. lain
12. lay
13. lies
14. lain
15. lay
16. lay
17. laid
18. lying
19. lying
20. lying
21. laid
22. laid
23. lies
24. Lay
25. lying
26. lay
27. laying

Page 66

1. sit
2. set
3. sit
4. set
5. Set
6. sits
7. set
8. sat
9. sit
10. sit
11. set
12. sit
13. sitting
14. sit
15. sat
16. sit
17. sat
18. set
19. set
20. sit
21. set
22. set
23. sitting
24. set
25. sit
26. sit
27. sets
28. sat, set

Page 67

1. teach
2. learn
3. teach
4. learn
5. teach
6. teach
7. teach
8. teach, learn
9. teach
10. teaching
11. learn
12. taught
13. teach
14. teach, learn
15. learn, teach
16. taught
17. teach
18. taught
19. taught
20. learning
21. teach
22. teaching
23. learned

Page 68

1. I
2. She
3. I
4. She
5. I
6. He
7. he
8. She, I
9. I
10. He
11. we
12. They
13. I
14. It
15. She
16. He
17. I
18. He and I
19. We
20. They
21. she
22. I
23. We
24. She
25. Sentences will vary.

Page 69

1. me
2. me
3. her
4. us
5. her
6. them
7. Vince and me
8. him
9. him
10. her
11. me
12. us
13. Tracy and me
14. us
15. them
16. me
17. us
18. him
19. me
20. him
21. them
22. us
23. her
24. him
25. them
26. her
27. us

Page 70

1. her, hers
2. his, mine
3. their, yours
4. her
5. their, theirs
6. his
7. his
8. our, its
9. their
10. their
11. its
12. My, our
13. its, our
14. its
15. her
16. her
17. your, mine
18. its
19. his
20. your, ours
21.–22. Sentences will vary.

Page 71

1. Everyone
2. somebody
3. Anything
4. Something
5. Everybody
6. No one
7. anyone
8. Both
9. Nothing
10. anybody
11. Someone
12. Everybody
13. Each
14. Some
15. Several
16. No one
17. Everyone
18. Nobody
19. Everything
20. anything
21.–28. Answers will vary. Possible responses:
21. Something
22. someone
23. No one
24. nobody
25. somebody
26. someone
27. anyone
28. Several

Page 72

Words in bold should be circled; other words should be underlined.
1. **Jenna/Rob**, their
2. **Jenna**, her; **Rob**, his
3. **friends**, they
4. **Rob**, he
5. **Jenna/Rob**, their
6. **Jenna**, her
7. **Jenna**, her
8. **cake**, it
9. **Sara**, she
10. **Rob/Jenna**, their
11. his
12. their
13. its
14. they
15. her
16. their
17. her
18. their
19. he
20. their

Page 73

1. themselves
2. herself
3. I
4. myself
5. himself
6. himself
7. We
8. oneself
9. themselves
10. itself
11. themselves
12. I
13. herself
14. himself
15. ourselves
16. me
17. I myself
18. me

Page 74

1. which
2. who
3. that
4. that
5. that
6. who
7. who
8. who
9. whom
10. Whoever
11. who
12. whom
13. who
14. whose
15. whom

Page 75

1. Who
2. Who
3. Whom
4. Who
5. Who
6. Who
7. whom
8. whom
9. Who
10. Who
11. Whom
12. Whom
13. Who
14. Who
15. Whom
16. whom
17. Whom
18. Whom
19. Who
20. Whom
21. who
22. Who
23. who

Page 76

Adjectives will vary. Possible responses:
1. brave
2. fragrant
3. cold
4. many
5. shiny
6. foolish
7. The, spicy, warm, the, small
8. A, gusty, the, wet, the
9. a, long, blue, the, new
10. clean, a, soft, warm
11. tired, a, long, the, huge
12. a
13. an
14. an
15. an
16. a
17. an
18. a
19. a
20. an
21. a
22.–23. Adjectives will vary.

Page 77

1. South American
2. African
3. English
4. Mexican
5. French
6. Russian
7. Puerto Rican
8. Roman
9. Alaskan
10. Canadian
11. Norwegian
12. Scottish or Scotch
13. Irish
14. Chinese
15. Spanish
16. Italian
17. Hawaiian
18. Japanese
19.–28. Sentences will vary.

Page 78

1. those
2. those
3. these
4. those
5. These
6. that
7. this
8. Those
9. those
10. that
11. those
12. these
13. Those
14. Those
15. that
16. these
17. this
18. Those
19. that
20. those
21. this
22. Those
23. these
24. These
25. that

Page 79

1. smoother, smoothest
2. busier, busiest
3. nicer, nicest
4. stronger, strongest
5. easier, easiest
6. bigger, biggest
7. kinder, kindest
8. calmer, calmest
9. rougher, roughest
10. narrower, narrowest
11. braver, bravest
12. shorter, shortest
13. happier, happiest
14. sadder, saddest
15. prettier, prettiest

Page 80

1. more interesting, most interesting
2. more dangerous, most dangerous
3. more professional, most professional
4. more important, most important
5. more difficult, most difficult
6. less helpful, least helpful
7. less practical, least practical
8. less serious, least serious
9. less enjoyable, least enjoyable
10. less beautiful, least beautiful
11. rainier
12. most faithful
13. more agreeable
14. busiest
15. longer

Page 81

1. injured
2. irritated, waiting
3. scampering
4. hidden
5. advanced, beginning
6. Biting
7. falling
8. singing, clapping
9. prepared
10. drooping, watering
11. waiting
12. aging
13. melted
14. moving, used
15. expanding
16. sliding
17. terrified
18. frozen, reflecting
19. commanding
20. painted, arriving
21. written, extended
22. grieving
23. growing
24. surviving
25. dedicated
26. Homing
27. whistling
28. Ironed
29. troubled
30. loving, comforting

Answer Key
Language: Usage and Practice HS, SV 1419027867

Pages 82–83

1. slowly, very, clearly
2. too, recklessly
3. slowly, quickly
4. too, harshly
5. there
6. well
7. suddenly, quickly, around
8. too, rapidly
9. pleasantly
10. soundly
11. noisily
12. really, early
13. severely
14. quickly, steadily
15.–22. Adverbs will vary.
23. slowly
24. very, quickly
25. too, early
26. patiently
27. very, cautiously
28. always, here
29. very, rapidly
30. swiftly
31. quietly, ahead
32. everywhere
33. now
34. slowly, well
35. extremely
36. always, carefully, never
37. far
38. here, neatly
39. quickly, sooner
40. very, fast
41. suddenly
42. softly
43. now, there
44. too, rapidly
45. there, extremely, very
46. very, politely
47. too, rapidly
48. extremely, well
49. Unfortunately, often
50. carefully
51. slowly
52. very, carefully
53. eagerly
54. recently
55. everywhere, yesterday
56. dearly
57. before
58. really

Page 84

1. sooner
2. soonest
3. hard
4. more
5. faster
6. most
7. sooner
8. faster
9. most
   frequently
10. more
    quickly
11. more
    seriously
12. earlier
13. hardest
14. more
    eagerly
15. faster

Page 85

1. of, for
2. through, around, on
3. through, from
4. by
5. At, to, about
6. among, with, for
7. beside
8. for, of, with
9. to, at, of
10. in, in
11. of, during, of
12. for, under, near, in
13. at, by
14. on, for
15. With, between
16. down, against
17. in
18. over, to, about
19. behind, between
20. Before, next to, in
21. across, in
22. over, into
23. After, of, under
24. below, of
25. into, above
26. During, out, across

Page 86

Words in bold should be circled.

1. (above the **clouds**)
2. (to a smaller **city**)
3. (on the second **block**)
4. (on that **hill**)
5. (on the wet **pavement**)
6. (in the seventeenth **century**)
7. (to the repair **shop**), (before next **week**)
8. (in **1781**)
9. (by **hand**)
10. (into the **street**)
11. (in a **pen**)
12. (over the **fence**)
13. (in a small **apartment**), (on **Dover Road**)
14. (to **America**)
15. (in **1847**)
16. (about **Sherlock Holmes**)
17. (of new **jobs**), (on the second **floor**)
18. (of the **United States**), (in **Kansas**)
19. (for **miners**), (by **Sir Humphrey Davy**)
20. (of **North Borneo**), (in **houses**), (on **stilts**)
21. (by the magician's **tricks**)
22. (in **Ontario**)
23. (in **New York City**), (in **1900**)
24. (into the vacant **house**), (for a quick **look**)
25. (in the **world**), (in **New York**), (in **1832**)
26. (of the **telephone**), (in **Scotland**)
27. (of the **radio**)
28. (of the giant **skyscrapers**)
29. (in the **waves**)
30. (by **Thomas Jefferson**)

Page 87

1. to the office supply store, adverb
2. in France, adverb
3. with the broken strap, adjective
4. to the public library, adverb
5. in an old house, adverb
6. with a printer, adjective
7. in the trash, adjective
8. in Myanmar, adverb
9. of my money, adjective
10. over the manager's instructions, adverb
11. of a Sequoia tree trunk, adjective
12. of New York State, adjective
13. near the docks, adverb
14. to the movies, adverb
15. in 1911, adverb
16. in this room, adjective
17. across the yard, adverb
18. for the new office, adjective, in the hall, adverb
19. across the lawn, adverb
20. around dark, adverb

Page 88

1. Neither, nor
2. and, not only, but also
3. but, or
4. but, both, and
5. not only, but also
6. Both, and, and
7. neither, nor, and
8. and, but
9. Either, or, and
10. although
11. Although
12. if
13. before
14. when
15. Unless
16. While
17. when
18. because
19. until

Page 89

1. their
2. they're
3. Their
4. there
5. their
6. they're
7. they're
8. their
9. there
10. their
11. their
12. they're
13. there
14. there
15. their
16. they're
17. there, their
18. They're, their
19. They're, there
20. They're, their
21. Their, there

Page 90

1. those
2. That
3. those
4. those
5. That
6. Those
7. those
8. those
9. these
10. those
11. these
12. these
13. those
14. this
15. Those
16. these
17. those
18. That
19. These
20. those
21. these
22. those
23. These
24. those
25. Those
26. this
27. This, that

Page 91

1. effects
2. affected
3. affect
4. effect
5. affected
6. effects
7. accept
8. accept, except
9. except
10. except
11. accepted
Sentences will vary.

Page 92

1. anything
2. anything
3. none
4. anything
5. any
6. any
7. anyone
8. any
9. any
10. no
11. anything
12. anything
13. any
14. any
15. nobody
16. any
17. any
18. anything
19. any
20. any
21. nothing
22. any
23. no
24. any
25. any
26. anyone
27. anybody
28. anyone
29. any

Page 93

1. plain
2. advice
3. past
4. quite
5. passed
6. lose
7. quiet
8. plane
9. advise
10. passed
11. loose
12. plane
13. lose

Unit 3 Test

Pages 94–95

1. common nouns: city, capital; proper nouns: Honolulu, Hawaii
2. proper nouns: Rainbow Natural Bridge, Utah
3. common nouns: composer; proper nouns: Igor Stravinsky, Russia
4. common nouns: niece; proper nouns: Jean, Thanksgiving

Language: Usage and Practice HS, SV 1419027867

5. women   11. candidate's
6. feet   12. A, reached
7. porches   13. A, Brush
8. sisters-in-law   14. A, won
9. children's   15. L, was
10. lawyers'   16. L, seems
   17. L, is
Words in bold should be circled.
18. **should have** remembered
19. **is** designing
20. **Did**, mop
21. **might**, arrive
22. **have** opened
23. **should, have** washed
24. me
25. themselves   27. my
26. me   28. He
Words in bold should be circled; other words should be underlined.
29. This, small, **comfortably**, last
30. The, large, **completely**, cleaning
31. **soundly**, the, howling
32. The, best, **easily**, the, finish
33. A, new, **recently**, the, gray
Words in bold should be circled.
34. (of **clothes**), (in the **laundry**)
35. (at a new **restaurant**), (near the **river**)
36. (of the **mountain**), (with **snow**)
37. (on the **corner**), (in one **week**)
38. (to the **office**), (with your **family**), (during your **vacation**)
39. C   41. D   43. B
40. B   42. A   44. D

Unit 4
Pages 96–97
Students should circle and capitalize the first letters of the following words.
1. once, i, poems
2. do, the charge, light brigade
3. british, titanic, england, united states
4. missouri river, pierre, south dakota
5. what, darrell
6. as, dave, the tonight show
7. the, american, george wythe

8. he, thomas jefferson, james monroe
9. the, the battle hymn, republic, julia ward howe
10. that, i, a league, their own
11. he, have, hoover dam
12. we, german, new ulm, texas
13. sequoia national park, sierra nevada mountains, california
14. i, william shakespeare, romeo, juliet
15. mayor myer, senator snivley, friday
16. dr. wolf
17. ms. lenore lindley
18. judge randolph
19. gov. luzer
20. mrs. carol creepton
21. supt. adams
22. mr. olden
23. chicago white sox, world series
24. houston astros
25. maj. stryker
26. s. carson st.
27. phoenix, az
28. oak ave., water st.
29. memphis, tn
30. col. clink, dover, nh
31. bentley boulevard, dover, nh
32. mason manufacturing, mason's mighty mothballs

Pages 98–99
Commas should be placed after words shown.
1. cotton, corn,
2. softball, races,
3. securely,
4. clear, accurate,
5. roof,
6. Alex, Frank, Candace,
7. steadily,
8. Gloves, goggles,
9. Alan, Carri, first,
10. cleaned, painted,
11. running,
12. Walking, running,
13. dinner,
14. corn,
15. battery, starter,
16. anyone,
17. typing, filing, shorthand,
18. peaches,
19. socks, sweaters,
20. sport,
21. application,
22. puzzles, games,
23. Diana, store, Justin,
24. Justin, sale,

25. Oh, 9:00,
26. earlier, Diana,
27. Yes, idea, said,
28. morning, Justin, crowd,
29. Anderson, dietitian,
30. First, diet,
31. Yes,
32. Well, habits,
33. Next, eat,
34. Anderson,
35. OK, question,
36. serving, Pierce, food,
37. example, student,
38. Class, group,
39. Carlton, nephew,
40. Montana, quarterback,

Pages 100–101
1. "Miss Allen, have you read this magazine article on getting your GED?" Karl asked.
2. "I'd like your opinion of what the article suggests," Karl added.
3. "Shannon, have you ever been to Rock Springs?" asked Dylan.
4. "It's a great place for a picnic," Dylan said, "and it has a pool nearby."
5. "Uncle Daniel, have you ever baked an apple pie?" Chad asked.
6. "Stella, how many members of the club are in this county?" asked Manuel.
7. "There are sixty active members," replied Stella.
8. "I have been saving money since I started keeping a budget," said Elena.
9. "Ava, I brought you a great book," Eddie said.
10. "We will learn to do spreadsheets next week," said Mr. Andrews.
11. "I'm going to plant the spinach just as soon as I get home," said Dee.
12. "When do we start on our mountain trip?" inquired Ernesto.
13. "You don't know," said our guest, "how happy I am to be in your house."
14. "My sister," said Jenny, "brought these beautiful baskets from El Paso."
15. "We will go to the park for a picnic," said Sandra.

16. "Will you carry this package for me?" asked Helena.
17. Did he surprise you when he said, "You can go home early"?
18. "Where is the nearest cafe?" inquired the stranger.
19. "Where are you going, Max?" asked his assistant.
20. "Stay right here," said Walt, "and I'll bring you the form you need."
21. "Guess who got the job," said Lorna.
22. "We have to get up early," said Ben, "if we want to see the sunrise."
23. I (After you read Chapter 4, "Going Nowhere," skip to Chapter 18, "Another Journey.")
24. C
25. C
26. I ("Steve, are you afraid?" she asked.)
27. I (My poem is called "If You Can.")
28. C
29. I (Amy told me, "You shouldn't have been concerned.")
30. C
31. I (Do you like the old Irish song called "Danny Boy"?)
32. C
33. I ("Have you read that computer book yet?" Sheila asked her friend.)
34. C
35. "Kim seems really distracted today," I said to Luisa.
36. "I know!" exclaimed Luisa, "It's as if she's not hearing anything I say!"
37. "I wonder if something is wrong," I said, "or do you think she's just thinking about the horror movie we saw last night?"
38. "I don't know if we can blame it on the movie," Luisa said, laughing, "but I do know she's been singing that song from the movie all day!"
39. "Did you hear her, too?" asked Luisa.

40. "Yes," I said, "and I started singing the song myself!"
41. "I played football with my kids all weekend," said Dave.
42. "So, did Jason make the team this year?" asked Karla.
43. "Yes, he did," said Dave, "and he can't wait for their first game."
44. "But I'm so sore I can hardly move today," Dave added.
45. Have you ever heard the expression, "You're only as young as you feel"?

Page 102
1. can't, homeowners'
2. can't, Seth's
3. You'll, days'
4. I've, Jeff's
5. Isn't, Porter's
6. didn't, Sue's
7. Haven't, Paul's
8. didn't, workman's
9. employees', didn't
10. officers', aren't
11. isn't, baby's
12. isn't, company's
13. Carla's, wasn't
14. captain's, navy's
15. company's, wasn't
16. Men's, Shannon's
17. women's, hasn't
18. aren't, Ann's

Page 103
1. neighbors; however,
2. TV; example,
3. tires; then,
4. maintenance;
5. enough; nevertheless,
6. help; result,
7. embarrassed;
8. money;
9. C
10. C
11. I (To begin, he decides on the kind of soldier and determines which kit he'd like to buy.)
12. I (Even though he uses a kit, his soldiers never look exactly like the kits do.)
13. C
14. C
15. C
16. I (Once I saw him crawl under his car; he was

trying to match the color of road dirt.)
17. C
18. Sentences will vary.

Page 104
1. 2:10
2. materials:
3. 4:30
4. Notice:
5. 3:00
8. Dear Ms. Thompson:
9. items:, items:
10. 10:00, choices:
11. note:

Page 105
1. fifty-one
2. customer-service
3. computer-software
4. sign-up
5. twenty-first
6. seventy-five
7. well-written
8. vice-presidents
9. A-plus, user-friendly
10. com-pute 14. en-close
11. sup-pose 15. fright-en
12. la-bor   16. out-side
13. hy-phen   17. cor-ner
Place dashes after words shown.
18. Suddenly— how—
19. (first) Maria— mean—
20. door— trembling—
21. Maria— matter—
22. out— lock—
23. things— incident—

Unit 4 Test
Pages 106–107
1. I   5. I   9. D
2. C   6. C   10. C
3. I   7. D   11. B
4. I   8. B   12. A
13. Capt. Margaret K. Hansen, Lakeview St., Phoenix, AZ
14. Jackson School, Wilson Stadium, Tues., Sept.
15. Gary L. Louis, M.D., Congress Rd., Syracuse, NY
16. Thanksgiving, Wed., Nov., Ms. Evans
17. I   19. C
18. I   20. C   21. C
22. Frank said, "Medicine helps to heal our bodies; music helps to heal our souls."
23. Cats have highly sensitive whiskers; consequently, they can

become agitated when something brushes against their face.
24. The label on the sweater told where the dress was made; it read, "Made in USA."
25. I'm certain she was born in Paris, Texas, not Paris, France, but let's call her to be sure.
26. Marcus did not begin the graphics class this semester; instead, he took a painting class.
27. B   29. A   31. B
28. C   30. A   32. A

Unit 5
Pages 108–109
Students should write *T* by these sentences.
1. Jack never has liked winter.
2. Smoking contributes to many health problems.
3. Computers are important in modern life.
4. A visit to a petting zoo is a good activity for children.
5. Collecting baseball cards is entertaining as well as educational.
6. Farmers owe a lot to George Washington Carver.
7. My favorite place to visit in Mexico is Guadalajara.
8. How can you pick a good child-care center?
9. He was, without question, the most adorable kitten Katya had ever seen.
10. The Arctic's climate is determined by the amount of heat and light received from the sun.
11. Jamal's computer had just shut itself off for no apparent reason.
12. Tyrannosaurus Rex was the largest of all meat-eating dinosaurs.
13. Mrs. Anaya's friends have an odd assortment of pets.

Pages 110–111
1. A 2. B 3. B 4. C
Students should underline these topic sentences.

5. Some people think California is not a safe place to live.
6. Other people think California is the best place in the world to live.
7. 1
8. 2   10. 2   12. 1
9. 2   11. 1   13. 2
Detail sentences will vary.

Page 112
Students should underline these sentences that do not belong.
1. The Chinese don't usually celebrate their birthdays the same way that people in western cultures do.
2. Hu-lan was named after her great-grandmother. Her father was an engineer.
3. Sometimes parents of young children talk with other parents who have children the same age as their own.
Paragraphs will vary.

Page 113
1. For example, also, At the same time, Furthermore
2. First, Then, Next, After that, After, Finally
Answers will vary. Possible responses:
3. therefore or consequently
4. for example
5. however, at the same time, or on the other hand
6. then, next, or after that
7. therefore or consequently

Page 114
1. 2, 3, 1, 5, 4
2. 3, 1, 2, 4 or 4, 1, 3, 2
3. 3, 1, 4, 2 or 4, 1, 3, 2

Page 115
Sentences may vary.

Pages 116–117
Sentences will vary.

Unit 5 Test
Pages 118–119
1. B   7. B   12. C
2. B   8. B   13. B
3. A   9. B   14. A
4. C   10. C   15. C
5. A   11. A   16. C
6. A